The Craziest Thing

Thomas DeLong

ISBN-13: 9781981129867
ISBN-10: 1981129863
Library of Congress Control Number: 2017918337
CreateSpace Independent Publishing Platform
North Charleston, South Carolina

Acknowledgements

Before you dig in and begin reading this book, I want to make it clear that I'm not an author. I've never had any intentions of writing a book in my life, and I don't want to write a book ever again. I wrote this book because God gave me a story I felt compelled to share. A story so incredible I could not have even come up with something so crazy with my own imagination. This story as it is written is not only a 100% accurate account for the events that lead to an incredible marriage to my wife, Larissa, but is the result of what happened when I finally learned to trust God fully with my romantic life, in whatever direction it might go.

Don't read this book expecting to find it extremely well written and assembled. Many sections may seem to be written at a 3rd grade level. As I previously mentioned, I'm not an author, but if any parts do seem to be well written, it's because I've had the awesome help of my wonderful wife, Larissa, and my incredible friends, Anna, Matt, and Jesse, as well as a handful of other friends who contributed and helped bring this project to fruition.

I hope many of you who read this find a lot of value in this story God gave me and will learn to trust Him to give you an incredible story of your own. Enjoy this story, and please don't ask me to write one ever again.

Philippians 4:11 (ASV)
"Not that I speak in respect of want: for I have learned, in whatsoever state I am, therein to be content."

The Craziest Thing

CHAPTER 1
On My Own

What's the craziest thing you've ever done? I've always had difficulty answering this question. After all, I wasn't your ordinary farm boy. I was an adrenaline junkie – a good one, too. Silos at the farm became my personal cliffs for rappelling, and the barn roof was, to me, an excellent cliff-drop substitute for snowboarding. In fact, the Pennsylvania snow came with crazy new ideas each year. Even the farm four-wheeler was put to good use for power-sledding: a terrifyingly awesome ride for every one of my friends, who sat down on the seat from a skid loader we bolted to a three foot saucer. This saucer was made of solid aluminum and cut from the end of a nitrogen tank, which we would then tow behind the four wheeler with a steel cable.

As time went by, my interest in adrenaline-fueled activities only increased. I had a close brush with death when I wrapped my car around a telephone pole at 100 MPH. The impact bent the entire frame of the car and I ended up with the pole right where the passenger seat was. The passenger door was forced flat against the dashboard in a way that it shouldn't ever be. It was as if Thor had slammed my door shut while he was having a bad day. After the accident, my family assumed I would be slowing down. I took it easy for a couple months as my fractured collarbone mended itself back together, but my desire for an adrenaline high came right back in time for me to prepare to finish high school and try to figure out what I wanted to do with my life.

Before I graduated, an elder from my church gave his testimony. He was a highly respected gentleman and I looked forward to hearing his story. His first words were, "Well, I've had a pretty ordinary life." My heart sank. After all my crazy endeavors the thought of an ordinary life seemed almost tragic – a thorough waste on someone as energetic as myself. I was positive that I would never find satisfaction with a normal life. I was about to graduate, and the thought of settling into normality was not even relatively close to being an option.

That night, while reflecting on the words I'd heard earlier, I sincerely prayed to God that He would not give me ordinary life, but something much greater. I craved adventure, adrenaline, and everything out of the extraordinary.

Shortly after completing high school, I set my sights on moving to California and pursuing a career in stunts. After all, it made sense to build a career around the things I loved to do anyway. While working long hours on the farm to save up money, I continued to build off of my current skills like rock climbing and snowboarding, and looked for any outlet I could find. I got my SCUBA certification, began working towards becoming a licensed skydiver, and even attended a couple of high-performance driving schools. Eventually, my fixation on my career goals led me to the International Stunt School in Seattle. At the stunt school I spent several hours training in stage combat, as well as how to use equipment such as air rams, which launched me into the air as if I was running from an explosion. I jumped 40 feet from a platform onto an airbag, which caught me unharmed, but did give me a headache. We also practiced wire acrobatics like you would see in movies like The Matrix. I was even set on fire - almost completely engulfed by flame, but safely and quite purposefully. I felt all this training, in addition to the skills I was already able to list on my resume, would give me the foundational skills necessary to have a well rounded career in the stunt industry, Going to this stunt school would give me the opportunity to learn how to use various equipment used for stunts, and acquire a few more skills along the way. Immediately afterward, I moved to California with the hope of breaking into the movie industry and becoming a stunt performer and stunt driver for film and television.

So what's the craziest thing I've ever done? That was certainly a very difficult question to answer. There were so many things to choose from.

So there I was, barely 20 years old making a new life for myself in Los Angeles. As I struggled to find work, my savings quickly dwindled. Just as I was about to run out of money, I learned how to make ends meet working as an extra. Besides the benefit of making money, it was also necessary for me to work as an extra so I could gain eligibility to join the Screen Actors Guild, which would allow me to be able to get work on big name film projects. Working as an extra was exciting. I had the opportunity to be a WWII soldier fighting in

The Pacific, a college student in How I Met Your Mother and saw Ted Mosby mistakenly teach in the wrong classroom, I spent an entire night screaming and running from Drones created by an evil mastermind in Iron Man 2, and I even had the opportunity to be a high-school student and stand in line with several other guys waiting to speed date iCarly.

When I wasn't working on different movie and television sets, I was going to the beach in Santa Monica, surfing in Orange County, or rock climbing in Malibu Creek. Another favorite place of mine was Point Dume, where I climbed right off the sandy beach and enjoyed the ocean views on the way up.

Even though I felt as though I was living the dream, there was a large aspect of the dream that was missing. I had made little to no progress on the dream I had set out to accomplish. Sure, I managed to work as an extra for several movies and TV shows, but I barely made any progress towards being eligible to join the union, which was necessary in order to do any stunt work for the big movies and tv shows. I wasn't anywhere close to achieving my goal. Not to mention the fact that Los Angeles was flooded with more talented adrenaline junkies who shared the same dream as I did. I was beginning to feel inadequate. As a 20 year old experiencing life off the farm for the first time, it was very difficult to adapt. My work as an extra slowed down progressively and as I had less and less money coming in. I made the best of things, but being completely broke for such an extended period of time absolutely sucked. I wasn't used to this concept at all. I'd been used to a solid income with few expenses since I was 12.

As time went on, the city grew more and more intimidating. I wasn't making any progress in what I had set out to do. In fact, I no longer felt the desire to have a career in the stunt industry. After several months working several different movie sets, the glamour completely faded, and my ambition had dwindled.

The idea of working on the farm didn't look so bad anymore. The idea of a steady paycheck and a comfortable living was starting to seem ideal to me. A career and a life of predictability and steady income. I wanted to get married someday and how would I be able to do that if I was broke with an unclear future?

As doubts about living in California continued to fill my mind, the idea of moving back to Pennsylvania became more and more realistic. Once I finalized my decision to move back, I called my dad and delivered what he would later describe as the best news he had ever heard in his life. I was coming home. I would be working on the farm again, living back with my parents. Even though I sometimes wish I could have a serious sit-down with my younger self about how I should stay in California and tough it out, I know that God's timing is always best. I remember being filled not with excitement, or feelings of discouragement about moving home, but with a strong sense of peace. It was what made sense in the moment, and where I felt God was leading me.

Since the decision was finalized in my mind about moving back to Pennsylvania, I knew the best thing I could do was make an epic road trip out of it. I reached out to my cousin, Jordan. Even though he lived in Michigan, we had developed a close relationship. He had spent several summers in Pennsylvania with my family, and we had several adventures together during those times.

Jordan was a few years younger than me and had just graduated high school. He was more than happy to join me for a road trip across the country when I presented the idea to him. His dad could not have been more supportive and even paid for his flight to California.

The next couple weeks were loaded with nothing but adventure. Before loading the car down with all my belongings and starting the actual trip across the country, we first did a tour of Northern California, visiting Yosemite, San Francisco, and seeing some of my family in Chico and Sacramento.

Upon our return to LA, we spent a week exploring the best of the city; doing some cliff jumping and rock climbing in Malibu Creek, checking out Hollywood and Venice, and hiking above Burbank and Glendale where we overlooked the city lights that spanned further than we could see.

After our enjoyable time exploring the gems of Southern California, we packed up my car with all my belongings and set off for the trip home. My Mitsubishi Lancer not only had a full trunk and backseat, but I had a roof bag on top to carry even more. We were putting all four cylinders to such hard work we had to turn off the A.C. anytime we drove up a hill.

The remainder of our trip was incredible as we checked out Las Vegas, Saw the sunrise at the Grand Canyon, experienced some refreshing showers in the mountains of Colorado, and spent a day seeing all the unique features of Yellowstone. After a long final stretch that included brief stops at Mt. Rushmore, the Badlands, and Chicago, we made it back to Michigan where we took a couple days to recuperate from some intense traveling.

It was time for me to drive the final stretch home Pennsylvania on my own. The twelve hour drive didn't seem all that bad after trekking the long way across the country. I made it back to my hometown of Quarryville, PA just in time to catch the last few hours of the annual Solanco Fair, which was just the culture shock I needed to remind me I was back home. I reflected on the last year of my life. What I had seen. What I had done. Where I had been. All before I had even turned 21. Life was about to revert back to an old normal. There were parts of LA I certainly was missing already, but I was happy to not worry about paying rent, or having to worry about how I was going to make ends meet. I could live comfortably again with steady work on the farm.

After having been through an epic year, I found that my life experiences had given me a way to make a profound impression on teenagers and I felt God calling me to find a way to get involved in youth ministry. It was something I had thought about in the past, but never felt strongly called to up until this point.

As I expressed how I felt about this calling to several of my friends, one of them invited me to a group called Young Life. It wasn't happening anywhere near my home, but they were planning to expand to Solanco, the school I had graduated from right down the road from my farm. Young Life was different than any other ministry I had ever seen before. The leaders were chill, they hung out with the teens as if they were their friends. During "club", they played silly games, sang along to pop songs you wouldn't hear on a Christian radio station, and then they talked about Jesus for 15 minutes as if the kids had never heard of him before.

This was brilliant. It was an approach that made so much sense to me: building relationships with kids who didn't know who Jesus was, and having designated time geared towards having fun and meeting them at their level. My interest spiked. I knew God wanted me to help this ministry start in Solanco.

One of the clear benefits to working on the farm was my flexibility to be involved in the ministry. I would visit them at school when I was on my lunch break, I'd be able to leave work early enough to pick up kids for club, and I would even meditate and prepare my lessons while I worked. I was also able to take them camping, rock climbing, and any other crazy ideas that came to mind. I poured my life into them. I was working on the farm 50-60hrs a week, while making time almost every evening to hang out with some of the guys I was mentoring. Looking back, I'm fairly certain, for the 3 years I volunteered for Young Life I was only half awake. Any current Young Life leader would completely relate.

After a few years of involvement, I found myself enjoying Young Life so much that I began to consider working for their ministry full-time. At the same time I couldn't help but wonder if a career change might help me meet the girl I'd spend rest of my life with. Up to that point I'd been interested in a handful of girls, but I'd received little reciprocation. I'd been out on my share of limbs and had crashed-and-burned an equal amount of times. It seemed as though the kind of girls I was into had no interest in dating a guy like me with a stable career in farming, regardless of the fact that I was so involved with ministry or had such a sense of adventure and a list of adrenaline-pumping hobbies.

Even though I wasn't having any progress with my love life, the belief that I'd one day be happily married remained constant. Making a career change started to sound like it might improve my odds of finding someone to partner with my in this adventure we call "Life."

As my interest increased in leaving the farm behind in the pursuit of full time ministry, I had the opportunity to meet weekly with Derrick. Derrick was only a year older than me, but leaps and bounds ahead of me in life. He was married with a kid, and another kid on the way. Not to mention, he was the Area Director for Young Life. A position I was hoping to attain within the next few years. As a spiritual leader, he took part of being a mentor. We would discuss what I'd been learning about God, my life, and what I saw in my future. One conversation in particular has remained very lucid in my mind. In frustration, I poured out my emotions pertaining to the desire for a lasting relationship. "I just don't understand it," I stated. "I have a steady income, a bright future, I volunteer my time in youth ministry, I'm adventurous, I'm fun, I'm pretty awesome all around! I just don't understand why it's so difficult to get a girlfriend."

Derrick, using all the wisdom in the room (I wasn't offering much), sat quietly for a few moments while pondering my situation in life. Then, with one question, he turned my world upside down. He lifted his head and slowly asked, "What if God doesn't want you to get married? What if He wants you to be single for the rest of your life? Have you ever thought about that?" The questions blew my mind. I was so accustomed to everyone around me giving reassurance that I would eventually find the right girl. I raised my eyebrows in disbelief as the concept of being single for the rest of my life slowly sunk in. I couldn't believe he even brought up such a foreign concept.

I quickly recovered from the shock and proceeded deeper into the conversation. "Some people are made to be single all their lives," I stated confidently. "But God made me to be married someday. There's no way God made me with this desire only to leave me single forever."

Here in front of me was Derrick, who married his college sweetheart at a young age and quickly started a family. I was convinced there was no way he could actually understand the position I was in– he already had everything I wanted.

As we parted he challenged me to ponder his insight. Though I agreed, I had no interest in considering the life he had insinuated, or exploring any further into the mere possibility of it. I remained adamant that God had created me for marriage and that I would find the perfect girl for me sooner or later.

Valentine's Day was approaching fast, and of course, I didn't have anyone to share it with. In fact, even with my strong desire for a relationship, I hadn't even had the opportunity to meet someone. Between working on the farm and volunteering my time with Young Life, my schedule was booked solid. While I was working in the barn, I came up with a brilliant idea. At least, it seemed brilliant in the moment.

The next time I was at the high school one morning, I pulled aside Luke. He was a sophomore that I had been mentoring and he was a small kid with blazing red hair, an irresistible personality, and he was liked by everyone, especially the girls. After discovering that he was free later that evening, I asked if he would like to go to the mall to do some Lady-ing. He laughed his usual laugh and stated that he had no idea what I was talking about.

"It's when you go somewhere intending to talk to some ladies," I coaxed innocently. "Here's what I'm thinking. You can be my wingman and go up to girls working in the mall and strike up a conversation. Find out if their Christian, ask some general questions to see if they're my type, and tell them you're waiting to meet your Young Life leader there. Then you talk me up, make them interested in me, and then I show up. Super easy."

Luke, seeing both the humor and challenge involved, readily agreed. He headed off to class and I headed back to the farm for work.

That evening Luke and I headed for the mall. My friend Jesse asked if I wanted to hang out later that evening, and since I did want to spend some time with him, I invited him to come help us.

Jesse was one of my original Young Life kids who had already graduated high school. His plans to join the Navy were drawing near, but he was still in town. He thought that the idea of "Lady-ing" was hilarious, and he loved the idea of being involved. We decided that he would play the role of scout – to scope out each store for the right type of girls.

The first establishment Jesse scoped out was Walk In Love, a Christian apparel store. I quickly received a text from him saying, "Too young." Obviously, it wouldn't be appropriate for me to date a girl the same age as my Young Life kids. Nor did I have any desire to.

He then scouted my favorite sports gear and apparel store, Eastern Mountain Sports, to no avail. Having decided that a bit more strategy was needed, we regrouped in another part of the mall. Luke and I arrived there first. We were aware that after hitting the two best locations to find a girl I would find common ground with, our chances of finding the right lady for me was dwindling.

Upon rejoining us, Jesse had some news. "You'd never guess who I saw," he started. "April and Schmidt! I guess they're out on a date tonight. I told them what we're trying to do here," he finished with a laugh.

April was my co-leader. Together, we had been leading Young Life at the high school for about three years. We were the only leaders at the school who had been there from the start. She had recently married a guy named Ryan, who went by his last name Schmidt. They were both about my age.

It was pretty random they happened to be at the mall, but I thought it would be fun to get together with them for a bit. "Let's go find them!" I exclaimed, and with that, we quickly headed to where Jesse saw them and we then caught up to April and Schmidt in the center of the mall.

Before I could say anything, she pointed her finger at me and shouted "You are pathetic!" She was furious, and I could see tears welling up in her eyes. My heart started beating uncontrollably. This was the last thing I had expected. "Using our Young Life kids to get a date for Valentine's Day?!" she exclaimed, angrily. "You are so pathetic!"

I was in complete shock, and so embarrassed to be yelled at in a crowded mall, and even in front of Luke and Jesse.

Trying to calm her down and shrug off her obvious concerns at the same time, I calmly responded to her. "What's the big deal?" I inquired. "We're just doing guy stuff and having fun. This is what guys do!" I looked over at Schmidt, who looked almost as baffled as I was. "Schmidt," I started again, "You don't see a problem with this do you?" He raised his shoulders and eyebrows while tilting his head in ambiguity. I had no doubt that he saw the humor in our attempt to find me a girl, but he had no intention of siding against April. I could tell he was doing his best to not be dragged into this and further ruin their evening.

It felt like a big deal was being made out of nothing and all I wanted to do was get out of there. "Well, whatever," I told April. "If you see a problem with this we're going to call it a night and head home. I don't see what the big deal is." My heart was still racing with embarrassment and confusion. Luke and Jesse were also experiencing a bit of shock. Even though we were all there to see it happen, we had a tough time believing that April had yelled at me like that.

We talked about it on the way home as I did my best to justify what we'd been doing. I made several jokes about what had happened, downplaying my desires to find a girl. "It's not like I *need* a girlfriend. I'm very content with where God has me." I said as I tried to convince myself I really *was* content and really *was* trusting in God's timing for my love life. "It would be especially difficult to do everything I do with Young Life if I had a girlfriend. I'm sure He has someone out there for me. But between work on the farm and Young Life, I don't have much opportunity to meet anyone."

Ultimately, I was clearly lying to myself as I pretended to portray an ability to be truly content and trust God rather than express any need for a romantic relationship in my life. I wanted to do my best to lead a good example for these guys, and I didn't want to come off as "weak" or "vulnerable", even though it was painfully obvious that I wasn't just discontent, I was determined to take matters into my own hands.

After I dropped Luke and Jesse off I headed back home for the night. I wasn't looking forward to getting up the next morning. I was supposed to pick up Luke again and take him to Campaigners, our weekly Bible study for Young Life, where we would be seeing April again.

When I arrived at Campaigners the next morning, April pulled me aside. "Hey," she began with sincerity, "I'm really sorry for the way I yelled at you last night. I shouldn't have done that, especially not in front of Luke. It set a really bad example."

The fact that she was willing to come to me and apologize meant a lot. It takes a lot of humility. "It's alright," I calmly responded. "I just don't feel like we did anything wrong last night, but I'll be praying about it more. And I can promise you I won't be doing that again. I really hate that I upset you like that."

That event caused me to deeply ponder what I truly wanted, along with what God might want me to do. I so desperately wanted to get married and have my own family, I had shaped my life around that concept to ensure it would happen. That was the biggest reason for moving back from Los Angeles – I could barely make ends meet, and I wanted to provide for a family of my own more than I wanted to pursue my own career ambitions and personal desires.

One verse I became very familiar with was Psalms 37:4. "Take delight in the Lord and He will give you your heart's desires." I believed that I had been delighting in the Lord for quite some time, and somehow my heart's desires had yet to be fulfilled. Isn't that supposed to be how this works?

I began thinking more critically of what God wanted for me. If I had a wife, would I be able to have as much time to focus on ministry? Or even at all? Would I be able to have my motorcycle, or rock climb every week?

I began pondering the concept of what my life might look like if I continued living my life in expectancy of something God hadn't even promised me. After all, it doesn't say in the Bible that every man is guaranteed a wife. What if God wanted me to be single all my life and I was just wasting my time preparing for a family that would never be? I began to think about everything I might miss out on. After all, in 1 Corinthians 7:7, Paul wishes that everyone could get along without getting married like him.

What if I was doing all these things in preparation of someday finding someone to be my wife, and marriage wasn't a part of God's plan for my life? I felt as though I was already missing out on so many opportunities by building my life around the concept of getting married someday. The thought of the several adventures and experiences I could have if I were to stay single swirled around in my head. With these thoughts, I suddenly experienced a realization of joy.

It's amazing how you can change your mindset and you realize how much opportunity you really have in front of you. Suddenly, I was once again seeking adrenaline. I decided I needed to disregard the concept of getting married someday, embrace who God made me to be, and find a way to use it for His glory.

My mind started reeling with thoughts of all the crazy things I could be doing. I had no idea what God's exact plan was, but I would have a blast in the meantime as I figured it out. I decided I would start skydiving in the spring and work towards getting a skydiving license. Maybe I would consider working my way toward BASE jumping.

I was always drawn to the incredible ability to jump off a cliff and freefall before pulling the parachute. Or, better yet, wearing a wingsuit and experience the true feeling of legitimate flying.

Up to this point all my crazy stories had been turned into exciting lessons, which attracted the attention of the kids I mentored at Young Life. Surely, God could use my crazy stories and new profound desire for adrenaline in some way for His glory. I began planning more travel, and more crazy adventures. Life was an open book and I was ready to make it the best it could be.

Suddenly life was incredibly exciting. I no longer felt the need to find a wife to make life awesome, and I had never before felt so free in my life. I felt as though God was showing me such a thrilling alternative to the life I had been so adamant about finding for myself. A life full of adventures I would have missed out on had I remained adamant about finding a relationship.

I began sharing my change in perspective with my closest friends. I frequently told them "I want what God wants. If He wants me to be single for the rest of my life, I'm going to embrace that and use it to glorify Him." I talked about Paul and his attitude toward the single life, and eagerly explained how I had been fighting God's will and was allowing myself to miss out on an electrifying lifestyle.

Looking back I'm so grateful to God for bringing me to a point where I was able to trust Him fully in every aspect of life – especially with my love life. Rather than trusting in Him to provide a wife, I was trusting Him to lead me wherever I was supposed to go. I knew He was much better at designing an incredible life than I could ever be. Embracing the fact that

He would guide me made all the difference, and a whole new world of opportunity had opened.

It reminds me of Genesis 22, when God asked Abraham to sacrifice his son as a burnt offering. God had promised him a son – a promise that took a long time in fulfillment. Even after his wife had become barren, God came through. After years of waiting, praying, and finally being given the son he had asked for, Abraham was then asked to sacrifice his beloved son as a burnt offering.

It blows my mind, but the Bible doesn't say anything about Abraham hesitating at all. The next morning he saddled up his donkey, chopped up the firewood and set off with his son. Can you imagine what Abraham might have thought? Can you imagine explaining to your son that God instructed you to sacrifice him as a burnt offering?

When it was clear that Abraham truly trusted God fully, and loved Him more than anything else, an angel of the Lord called out from Heaven at the very last moment commanding him to stop what he was doing. It's as though God was was saying to Abraham "You know that Son, you prayed for, waited for, and I had finally given to you? I want you to give him to me. Let go of him, and give him to me."

Looking back, I feel as though God put me through a similar test. Of course, it wasn't nearly as extreme or dramatic, but I can see the Lord saying, "You know those desires you have for a wife and kids? Give them to me. Let them go."

Fortunately, I listened. I let go of those desires and stopped looking. I stopped wondering, and I stopped waiting. For the first time, I was fully content in where God had me in life, and wherever God may be taking me.

What's really crazy is that only two weeks later, God came through for me just like He did for Abraham. On March 2nd, 2013, I met a girl. And that's when things really got interesting.

CHAPTER 2
The Gamechanger

Sometimes it takes a while to come to terms with the cards we're dealt in life. Once we've learned to accept them God hands us a wild card out of nowhere, changing the trajectory of our lives forever.

It was my friend Travis's 21st birthday and so I took him out, along with our friend Drew, to celebrate this milestone. Travis is a short and stocky kind of guy. He always has a great sense of humor and, for some reason, at the time he idolized Usher. He's one of the older Young Life students that I've stayed in contact with over the years. He graduated High School a couple years prior and our friendship didn't end there.

Drew, who was also one of my Young Life guys, had graduated a year before Travis, when Young Life was just getting established at the high school. Drew is a classic straight-up hipster. At the time, he had curly hair, glasses, and he always articulated his words carefully.

The three of us were at a restaurant enjoying our time together when Drew received a text. He then proposed an idea that was about to make the night far more interesting. "Hey! My friend Larissa is in town! She's thinking about moving here and she wants to get acquainted with some new people. She's totally awesome and lots of fun! Is it okay if she joins us?" It sounded like a fun idea to me, but I didn't want a guys night to be ruined if that was what Travis was intending for this to be. I looked over to him and asked, "It's up to you. It's your birthday."

Travis had previously done a trip to New Hampshire with Drew and had briefly met Larissa when they were on that trip. Travis knew she would be a great addition to the evening and was quick to agree. Drew told her we would come by soon to pick her up.

It turned out that Larissa was at a townhouse she was planning to begin renting in a few weeks, and had traveled down from upstate New York to finalize the paperwork for the lease. It was only a few minutes away from the restaurant, so we headed her direction as soon as we paid our bill.

Larissa and Drew had attended Fairwood Bible Institute together in Dublin, New Hampshire. It wasn't your typical college - it was a conservative school tucked away in a beautiful territory facing a well recognized peak called Mount Manadnock. They had a strict dress code that all the students were required to adhere to. The Institute operated as a work study program where the girls and boys learn individual vocational skills, in addition to their biblical studies. During the three year program, Drew only attended for a single semester and Larissa had attended a year and a half. During their overlapping time there, they had come to be good friends.

Drew, Travis, and I walked up the steps toward her town-house. It was located in an urban, but less busy part of the city. I was dressed up in my nice suit and power-tie. I was a big fan of How I Met Your Mother, and Barney Stinson was the inspiration behind my suit revelation. My suit was a slim-fitting black two button with contemporary lapels - a modern classic. I had also chosen a white shirt and my blue power-tie. It wasn't an ordinary tie. It was thick with woven silk that subtly highlighted a beautiful cross-hatch of blue and black. It felt expensive. And, teamed with my carefully groomed hair, it made me feel like a real winner. I didn't dress up nice for the sake of meeting anyone, but I was sure it would give me an edge.

We all walked up to her door and Drew gave it a few solid knocks. After a few moments Larissa opened the door while talking on her cell phone. She looked nothing like I had pic-tured in my mind. She was sock footed, dressed in jeans, with a casual long-sleeved blue shirt and her hair was thrown up in a careless ponytail. Even though she wasn't dressed to impress, she was striking. Her strawberry-blonde hair shimmered in the lamp light. Her wide and contagious smile reminded me a lot of Julia Roberts. With a bright smile that revealed two dimples, one on either side, she ushered us in. She was in the middle of her phone call and quietly told us she would be finished momentarily and encouraged us to make ourselves comfortable. When her conversation was over, she hung up the phone and Drew introduced us. After a few moments of brief introductions, we all hopped in my Subaru.

As we headed down the road, I was absolutely captivated by her energy and enthusiasm. She was up for just about any-thing. Her imagination was impressively creative, which was likely the result of growing up on a small farm with seven siblings, and having a limited number of things around them for entertainment. I learned that she was from a small town called Gilboa, which was in the middle of nowhere. They didn't have cable TV, so their entertainment was only limited to their ingenuity. Larissa revealed herself to be skillful storyteller. She painted for us a vivid portrayal of her life and her road trip to Lancaster. It's hard to describe how she tells a story. It's as if she throws her whole self into the act. Using hand gestures, animated facial expressions, multiple voice impressions and sound effects. As our conversations rolled on, I did my best to play it cool, but I knew I had never met a girl as electric as her.

She held my attention the entire evening and I couldn't help but be intrigued by all of her attractive qualities. In the brief time that she had been hanging out with us, I found her to be incredibly funny, entertaining, quirky, easy going, and adventurous. I was definitely interested in getting to know her better, and at the same time, I wanted to embrace the lessons that God had recently been teaching me. No matter what I did, I wanted to make sure that I was trusting Him.

We were only out for a few hours, but we all had a great time. We sang, danced, and carried on. Through all these crazy situations, it was clear that she wasn't afraid to be herself. In fact, it seemed as though the only thing she knew how to do was have fun and try to include everyone around her in her infectious laughter. She danced without a care in the world as she pulled off sweet dance moves like "The water sprinkler" and "Milking the cow" and the Larissa Original: "Collecting eggs while reading the bible". She told us what she was doing as she introduced us to all these new dance moves. Being a connoisseur of good times, I thought that was excellent.

At some point in the evening she turned to me and asked, "So you're the Tom that Drew always talks about? The one who builds the super large bonfires and does stunt driving?"

I laughed. "Yeah, that's me." I had no idea that he had bragged about me in such a way. "I'm not a very well established stunt driver, though. Maybe he gives me more credit than I deserve. I've only had one legitimate stunt driving gig and that was in Boston back in November."

"Everybody thinks I'm a bad driver because I wrecked two cars in six weeks," she smirked. "But they weren't my fault! The first one I was run off the parkway by a U-Haul truck, which wasn't allowed on the Parkway in the first place, and the second one I flipped my Eclipse because the road was snowy and I hit a patch of black ice under the snow, my car flipped upside down in a deep ditch and a snowplow literally plowed snow over top of my car before realizing I was even there!!" as her sentence had run on without taking a breath, she rolled her eyes as she took a large breath.

I laughed and replied, "You're not the only one. I wrecked two cars in six weeks as well. Some people would say I'm a bad driver, but I've just pushed the envelope too many times. I've learned to take it a little easier."

We shared our harrowing driving stories for a few minutes, laughing about our experiences. Did this girl really love fast cars and adrenaline-packed driving? She definitely had my attention. I began considering the possibility of asking her out on a date. After all, she was exactly my type and it seemed we had several things in common.

Larissa's phone started ringing so she briefly excused herself and walked away as she picked up her phone. I noticed Drew standing nearby observing our conversation. We were good friends, and I didn't want to do anything that might upset him. I knew he had always talked very highly of Larissa, but he never expressed any feelings for her. To be sure, I inquired if there was anything romantic going on between them.

He quickly responded, "No, we're just good friends. There's nothing happening between us."

"So do you mind if I go for it?" I asked cautiously.

Without hesitation he replied, "Not at all, but just so you're aware, she does have a boyfriend." Drew looked over to where she stood talking into her phone. After a second or two he turned back to me. "I don't think it's really a healthy relationship, but something you should at least be aware of."

"Alright," I nodded. The possibility of her being in a relationship didn't deter me. After all, I had *just* learned to fully trust God with whatever might happen in my love life. If nothing would materialize, I would carry on with life as usual, but if God had a place for her in my life, surely He would pave the way for such a thing to happen.

Not long after she came back, we decided to call it a night. I quietly convinced Drew to let me drop him and Travis off at his car so I could take Larissa back to her apartment to spend just a little bit of time with her alone. As I drove her home we were able to get to know one another outside of a group setting. She was just as energetic in a personal conversation as she was when we were with Drew and Travis. I honestly don't recall what we had talked about, but we just clicked. She wasn't like any other girl I had ever met.

Even though she piqued my interest and had my attention, I didn't forget what God had recently taught me. I was going to embrace whatever His plan might be, even if this girl might not be part of His plan.

I walked her to the door, as any gentleman would. I was really hoping for another chance to see her before she went back to New York. "Do you have any plans for church tomorrow?" I asked.

"I haven't decided for sure yet", she responded. "But I'm thinking about going to my roommate's church, The Worship Center, since she's invited me"

"Would you be interested in going to my church? It's only about 20 minutes from here." I tried to be as casual as I could. I didn't want it to seem as though I was asking her out on a date or anything too intimidating.

"Yeah, possibly." she responded sincerely.

"Alright, sounds good. What's your phone number? I'll shoot you a text in the morning and you can let me know" I said, still trying to play it cool. I didn't want her to think I was just asking for her number, which is exactly what I was doing.

She gave it to me without hesitation and on the inside I was feeling accomplished. I didn't think it could have gone any better. I wished her a good night as she stepped through her door.

I walked back to my car and began the drive home. When I made it home, I texted her so she would have my number. She responded immediately and we texted back and forth for a considerable amount of time. Her personality was even reflected in her text messages. I could almost feel her energy through my flip phone. I wished her a good night via text. Before I went to bed I quickly found her on Facebook and sent her a friend request. I did my due diligence and noted that she didn't have a significant other in her profile picture. It was a selfie of her smiling while holding a little girl. I looked in the "About Me" section and found she was listed as single. I excitedly concluded that she had broken up with her boyfriend and that the news simply hadn't reached Drew yet. After all, she never mentioned anything about him the entire evening. If she was in a relationship, it would definitely say so on her facebook profile, right? Her profile pic would definitely showcase her with a guy if she was in a relationship, too. With only light research I couldn't find any evidence at all about her having a boyfriend. I tried to shrug it off without overthinking it. I was beat, and what I needed was some sleep.

I laid down but I wasn't able to fall asleep immediately, as thoughts were swirling around in my mind. This girl was awesome. There was something strikingly different about her. I really wanted to keep myself in check and trust in what God had in store for me. I had finally become very fond of the idea of singleness, and yet, at the same time, I wanted to get to know this girl. I certainly found her more interesting than any girl I had ever met. I confidently decided to trust in God however things might turn out. I wanted what God wanted, whatever that may be.

The next morning I woke up and looked at my phone. There was a message from Larissa. "You have a CAT??!!! I knew you were awesome, but I didn't know you were awesome enough to have a cat!" It was obvious that she had been Facebook stalking me, which seemed like a good sign.

I crawled out of bed and hopped on the computer to check my Facebook. I had well over a dozen notifications. She had "Liked" several of my profile pictures, even my old ones. She was digging deep into my profile, and that was totally okay with me. With a huge boost of confidence, I sent her a text as I said I would. "So are you interested in coming to my church?" I texted her doing my best to seem aloof. A minute later my phone buzzed with a text.

"I'm going to The Worship Center with my roommate, but I can definitely check yours out sometime when I move down here." She replied.

Though I was slightly disappointed I wouldn't get to see her again before she went back to New York, we continued to text, making small talk throughout the day. A few times I sent open-ended texts in case she was looking to end the conversation, but she kept responding with enthusiasm. Naturally, this was exactly what I was hoping for. This girl was compelling, fascinating, and completely absorbing. I couldn't help but want to know more about her.

That afternoon I went to my grandparents to celebrate my Grandma Lehman's birthday with the rest of the extended family. As Larissa and I continued texting I was careful not to respond immediately to every text so I wouldn't come off as desperate.

"You better prepare for my awesomeness to return to Lancaster," one of her texts read. I had never encountered a girl with that kind of boldness. It was clear that we both had large egos and weren't afraid to unleash them. Lately I had been trying to curb my egotistical nature, but since she wasn't giving any signs of reigning hers in I wasn't about to be beaten.

"Well, you'd better watch out, cuz I'm the most awesome thing that ever happened to Lancaster," I replied back. I was slightly nervous about having said it. After all, an egotistical statement like that would come off the wrong way to any other girl I had ever known. But my confidence was at an all-time high, and I was curious how she would react.

Not even a minute later I received another surprisingly bold text. "You might be the most awesome thing to happen to Lancaster, but I'm the most awesomest thing that God put on the planet. God made the earth and it was good. God made me, and all He could say was "wow" because He had outdone Himself on me. I know. Because He told me so :)" the text read.

I was stunned. This girl thought she was even more awesome than I did. I pursed my lips, raised an eyebrow and nodded my head as I pondered the bold text I just received. "Okay," I thought to myself. "It's on."

Clearly this girl thought highly enough of herself to say such a thing. There was a part inside of me that legitimately believed her. In the past I had actually joked with my friends about how difficult it was to find a girlfriend because of how tough it was to find a girl awesome as I was. To me, the statement made complete sense. I was well-accomplished and had achieved some remarkably awesome things in my life. Of course it seemed impossible I'd find a girl that could strike me as intriguing.

The ensuing conversation with her was hilarious. I showed my brother and a couple of my cousins. They thought it was funny, but not quite as funny as I did. I couldn't tell if they were amused or slightly worried, but I had never heard a girl talk with such confidence before.

The next day my family and I went out to eat in the evening to celebrate a birthday. Larissa and I were still texting back and forth, and our conversation was still continuing to keep me entertained. We kept each-other informed of how our day was going and what we were up to.

"I'm out to eat with my family right now eating some delicious steak," I texted.

"That sounds awesome, I love steak!" she quickly replied. I sensed an opportunity to casually get her to commit to something small.

"How about I take you out for some steak sometime after you move down here?" I asked in effort to seem nonchalant, but still manage to land a date for when she returned. After all, she seemed totally interested.

Sometimes guys can feel like they're being crystal clear about making a move but it doesn't come across that way. I later learned that Larissa was convinced this was just going to be a friendly encounter with no romantic motives. After all, she wanted to make new friends in the area. At the same time, I was probably too vague, and was too excited at the prospect of having a date with this fascinating girl.

A couple days went by and the texts kept flowing. The conversation seemed to seamlessly continue as the week progressed. I admit that I was wholeheartedly looking forward to our date - at least what I thought was a date. But the longer I thought about it, something just didn't add up right. At the time I couldn't put my finger on exactly what it was, but the thought of simply taking the "most awesomest thing God put on the planet" out on a date as if she was just any ordinary girl, wasn't making any sense to me. I actually felt uncomfortable about the concept.

Why would I take the most awesome girl in the world out on an average date as if she's just any other girl? After all, she did declare herself to be the "most awesomest thing God put on the planet." And while she may have been joking, something inside me was convinced I should take her word for it.

As the thought of taking her on an ordinary date began to make my stomach churn, my mind began to wander about what might be a cool idea. I'm not sure how the idea got into my head initially. Maybe it was that I hadn't eaten dinner, and I was craving a juicy Double Double from In-N-Out Burger at the moment, but I thought about how awesome it would be to take her to LA for our first date. After all, if she's as awesome as she says she is, she would definitely be up for this. The more I pondered the concept, the more I liked it.

Just for fun, I hopped on my computer and got on Priceline's website. I wanted to tease myself with this outrageous concept and see how much the cheapest ticket prices from any nearby airport to Los Angeles would be. Not to buy a ticket, necessarily, but I enjoyed toying around with just the concept of this silly idea. Sure enough, I managed to stumble upon two round trip, non-stop tickets out of Dulles Airport in Washington DC for $250 each - leaving in 5 weeks. The flight left on a Friday and departed LA late Sunday night, arriving back in Dulles early Monday morning. Perfect for a quick, fun weekend.

This was an incredible deal. So incredible it was difficult to simply pass it up. Even though the thought had entered my mind initially as something that would be a wild, out-of-this-world-crazy idea, something about it made sense. Thoughts kept whirling around my mind of how awesome it would be to take her out to California for a weekend on our first date. From anyone else's perspective it probably seemed completely illogical, but to me, it made perfect sense. If there was any girl that I had ever known that would be up for this, I knew it'd be her. I felt so much more comfortable with the concept of taking her to Los Angeles for our first date than Texas Roadhouse. I thought about all the times I had been asked about the craziest thing I'd ever done. "This could be that thing!" I thought to myself as I continued to ponder this concept. I was feeling more and more comfortable with it. The pieces of the puzzle were all coming together. This was most certainly what I was going to do.

I called up Larissa. This would the first time I was actually speaking to her, rather than texting, since the night we met, so I decided to keep it simple. "Hey Larissa, how's it going?" I asked. We exchanged pleasantries as I guided the conversation to my purpose for calling. "I've been thinking about how we had talked about going out for steak when you move here. There's actually another restaurant I'd like to take you to. It's really good, and I think you'll like it, but it would take an entire weekend." Of course this other place in my mind was the legendary west coast In-N-Out Burger… In California.

"What is it, an all weekend buffet?!" She replied in laughter. Of course what I was saying to her didn't make any sense.

"Not exactly, but it'll be totally worth it. We'll meet some of my friends there and It'll be a lot of fun! I'm sure you'll like it," I told her. "But I just need you to promise me you won't schedule anything from April 12th to the 15th."

Larissa readily agreed with great curiosity as I continued. "I need you to promise me you won't schedule anything during that time. If you do manage to find a job right when you move down, just tell them you have plans for that weekend, and they'll have to honor that. I just need to make sure you're 100% going to follow through with this." I did my best to express how serious I was without being intimidating. The last thing I needed was for her to back out and I would then lose the money on the plane ticket.

"Oh, well.. Okay" she laughed. "Sure, I promise," She responded sounding intrigued. "Just don't tell me what it is, okay? I like surprises!"

"Sure, I can do that." I replied. I couldn't help thinking about how genuinely surprised she was going to be. "*It's a good thing she likes surprises,*" I thought to myself, "*because this one is going to blow her mind.*"

We said our goodbyes as I walked back into my house and logged back onto to my computer. I had been talking in my car, since I was still living with my parents at the time. This was certainly not a conversation I wanted them to overhear. I was sure they would question my sanity if they caught wind of what my plan was.

I sat back in my recliner and picked up the keyboard. I went back onto Priceline to look up the tickets again. My phone buzzed with a text from Larissa. "This weekend thing had better be awesome."

"Don't worry" I texted back as a grin widened on my face. "I'm sure you won't be disappointed." She had no idea how not-disappointed she was going to be.

I found the tickets and purchased them without hesitation. I reserved a rental car as well and booked a place to park my car for the weekend at a Hilton Hotel near the airport.

Meanwhile, Larissa and I continued making small talk and texting back and forth. It was pretty late, and I had work early in the morning, but I was feeling bold after putting my plans into motion. "Goodnight, Beautiful." I texted to her. After all, it wasn't the boldest thing I had done all day.

"I'm not beautiful -_-" she texted back. Now I was stuck. I couldn't just let the conversation end there. I've never heard of a girl saying such a thing and "OK" be an acceptable response.

"Don't make me sing One Direction. I will if I have to." I texted back. The song "That's What Makes You Beautiful" was pretty high up on the charts at the time.

"Haha alright. Well have a good night," she replied.

I texted a simple "Goodnight" and laid down still feeling confident. I knew that this was going to the greatest date of all time. I prayed to God that everything would work out as I went to sleep. This date was only 5 short weeks away and I had a lot to look forward to.

CHAPTER 3
Let's Just Be Friends

The next morning I woke up with every bit of enthusiasm I went to sleep with. After eating a healthy breakfast, I started my morning routine of feeding the cows on the farm. I continued to imagine how awesome this first date was going to be. As I kept myself busy mixing feed in the large farm equipment, my phone buzzed with another text from Larissa. Her text came in later than usual, which had me loaded with even more anticipation, especially with the way our texting ended the night before.

I flipped my phone open in hopes of reading something that would reciprocate the bold text I had sent previously. "Hey Tom, I just need to be sure we're on the same page with things." It read. "I'm seeing somebody.. I can only go on this weekend thing if it's not a date and we just go as friends, is that ok?" A part of me wants to say my heart sank, but honestly, I was only mildly disappointed. I pondered this new information briefly before shrugging it off. I was still on a pretty serious confidence high: the kind of absurd confidence that kills young guys on motorcycles.

"It's totally cool." I replied casually. "We can totally still go as friends." In my head, I was talking to myself sarcastically. *"I mean, yeah. We can totally fly to California for a weekend just as friends. That's totally something that friends do. There's nothing odd about that. Going as friends is only slightly more crazy than going as our first date."*

It was certainly disappointing to receive the confirmation that she was in a relationship, and Drew had been right all along. However, even though Larissa was telling me she was in a relationship, I was confident it wasn't going to last long. I could tell her heart wasn't in it, since she didn't mind texting me so often ever since we had met. She wasn't putting off the reserved "I have a boyfriend" vibe. Besides, her Facebook profile didn't say she was in a relationship. Any time a girl is in a relationship she's excited about, that is the first thing she changes.

I knew I had time to change things around. After all, if she really liked this guy, she would have said something about him early on, and she probably wouldn't be so enthusiastic about moving away from him either. She gave me her number the night we met and we had been texting ever since. I couldn't help but feel the odds were stacked against him and were very much in my favor. She still had three weeks until she moved down, and then this "weekend thing" was only two weeks after that. I had five full weeks to turn this around and I felt as though I was in pretty good shape.

I still couldn't help but be stoked about this idea. Even though I had just purchased airline tickets and reserved a rental car for what I thought was going to be a date, somehow this news didn't phase me one bit. The confidence I had in life at the time was reaching an all time high. Something deep inside told me this absurd concept of a date was going to work and nothing could convince me otherwise.

I excitedly texted some of my closest friends to tell them about my plan. Of course I still called it a date and left out the part that she still had a boyfriend. They really didn't know what to think. Some of them thought I was crazy, others told me it was a bad idea, and if she was willing to go somewhere with me for a weekend, she probably wasn't the kind of girl I should be dating. Of course, I understood how this could easily sound promiscuous, however I at least knew her well enough to know this was not the case.

On the back end of this whole idea there were a few minor details working together, making this concept far less questionable than it may have seemed to be on the surface. Honestly, if this was a random girl that I had met on my own, it would be all kinds of sketchy. Given the fact that we had a mutual friend, Drew, who knew both of us very well, I was able to trust that she was the Christ centered person he described her to be. Likewise, Larissa was able to trust that I was an upright guy who had a deep relationship with Christ as well, just as I presented myself to be. When Drew went to Fairwood Bible Institute, I was one of his friends he talked highly of, given my past in stunt driving, and work as a movie extra. Even though I was his Young Life leader for a short time, I had made quite the impression upon him. He was unknowingly working as my wingman, setting me up for one of the biggest stunts of my life; my first date with Larissa. The mutual connection Larissa and I had with Drew made all the difference between making this a great idea versus a horrible idea.

Another factor that worked perfectly was the fact that I had lived in Los Angeles for over a year. To me, it was a second home. I wouldn't have been comfortable taking her somewhere I hadn't been before or where I didn't know anybody. I had friends in LA, and we would be spending most of our time with them. They would be sure to provide separate sleeping arrangements for us, since we were both strongly committed to saving ourselves for marriage. I wouldn't want it any other way. I really did look forward to showing her all of my favorite places, as well as being able to introduce her to my friends on the left coast.

As I worked hard completing numerous tasks on the farm, my day eventually slowed. I had to get rye out of the silo, which meant to monitor it coming out of the silo and watch for any breakdowns. I typically used this time to read, or even prepare lessons for young life. As long as everything was working well mechanically, this was always excellent down time. As I processed the recent chain of events that had lead me to plan such an extravagant first date, my eyes widened with a huge realization: I had only known this girl for five days. She was only in my presence for three hours. Who is this girl? Did this girl really leave such an incredible impression in a short amount of time that had inspired me to buy airline tickets, reserve a rental car, and put so much on the line? I was astonished. She certainly had a blazingly extravagant personality and I had never met anybody in my life that ever affected or inspired me in that way. She was really awesome, and that I knew for sure. I knew if she was as awesome as she claimed to be, this was the right thing to do. I had no doubt in my mind.

In the following weeks, Larissa and I stayed in touch. We continued our phone correspondence back and forth as our conversations became a routine part of our day. One evening while I was on my way to a Bible study, we were texting and something about the tone of her texts seemed slightly off. They weren't radiating the typical energy they usually did. I asked her if everything was ok and she told me her boyfriend was really upsetting her, and she was incredibly frustrated with him.

Here was my chance to sweep in and be the hero. This was something any guy would do to gain the trust of a girl. I find it surprising how many times guys do this and the girl's first instinct is that they're just being a good friend. Such innocence.

"Would you like me to call you later and we can talk about it?" I asked her in the text.

"Sorry, this is really bothering me a lot and I just don't want to talk about it." She replied.

"How about I call you and we'll talk about other things so I can help get your mind off of it?" There it was. I was baffled at how smooth and brilliant I really could be.

She agreed--I was in. I called her when I got home and we talked for about an hour and a half about anything and everything. I talked about how I had lived in California and all the exciting things that were out there and how much I missed it. I found it to be very enjoyable to talk to her. Conversation came very naturally. Everything about her was incredible. Even over the phone she didn't simply talk like any other person would. I could tell she was talking with her hands and using several unique facial expressions to match whatever voice impersonation she was using at the time.

"As you know, I nanny for a family who has a two year old little girl, and an eight year old girl. Where I nanny, I don't have any cell service, so I just use their wifi. That's why you don't hear from me as much during the day. I have to go to the window, hold my phone upside down and shake it in order to get a text to send."

I could tell she was physically pretending to hold her phone upside down in her hand and begin shaking it as she described it to me.

"Wow, life must be difficult living in the middle of absolutely nowhere. So I guess it makes sense I mostly hear from you on facebook during the day." I said.

"Yeah, a certain someone" she began as she coughed a couple fake coughs into her fist "gets seriously upset when he doesn't hear from me through the day."

She was obviously referring to her boyfriend, who was sounding more and more like bad news. This guy certainly sounded like he didn't deserve a girl as awesome as Larissa.

The conversation began steering into the direction she was wanting to avoid. However, allowing her to vent to me about the frustrations she was having with her boyfriend not only helped her blow off some steam, but I was able to better understand her current situation.

I heard her sigh over the phone. The sigh in and of itself spoke volumes.

"Hey, so about earlier…" She started. "I want to apologize if I came across rude or crabby. I've been dealing with a lot lately and I let it get the best of me for a moment there and I'm sorry."

"It's alright." I told her. "I could tell something had been slightly off, but I'm glad you can be open about what's going on. Just let me know if you need someone to talk to, and I'm always happy to be here. Whether you want to talk about something specific, or just get your mind off things. Let me know." I wanted to further open the door for more conversation in the future.

Larissa then opened up about how she was wanting her current relationship to end. She hated the idea of breaking up with someone and was pretty much waiting for him to break up with her.

This was music to my ears. I encouraged her to break up with him if it wasn't what she wanted. I told her that letting it slide over time, just tends to get messy and difficult. I suggested ending it quickly and efficiently, like ripping off a band-aid to get it done and over with, as I discussed the merits of a clean-cut end to a relationship.

She agreed with my reasoning, yet held onto the hope that he would break up with her, since she didn't want to hurt his feelings. Meanwhile, I clung to the hope she wouldn't have a boyfriend by the time she moved to Lancaster, or especially by the time I took her to California. Our conversation ended well as we said goodnight. After we hung up, we texted a few more times before going to sleep. She sent me a text saying "Goodnight. Thanks for talking to me tonight."

A week later, I woke up in the morning and read a text she had sent me. She had finally put an end to the relationship.

"I'm sorry to hear that :-/" I replied. That was a lie. I wasn't sorry, I was overjoyed. If I *was* sorry for anything, it would be the fact that she had to put herself through an unpleasant conversation. That was one less obstacle to worry about in ensuring everything went well for this first date, which in my mind, I was confidently still considered to be a date. I wasn't worried about whatever she was calling it. To me, it was a date. It was easier to call it that, at least.

I texted Drew and told him Larissa had broken up with her boyfriend. My prediction that her heart wasn't in the relationship had proven to be accurate. He didn't respond for a long time, but when he did, he asked if I could join him and Travis for pizza that evening. I agreed and met with them that night.

I arrived at the pizza restaurant and sat down with them. Something felt slightly different, but I carried on the conversation with them anyway.

As great of a friend Drew was, I hadn't told him about my plans for the first date. He was too close to Larissa, and for him to have any knowledge of it was just far too risky. Of course I had to tell his younger brother, Cameron, who had come to be a close friend of mine as well. Cameron had actually agreed to join me for the weekend in California if my plans with Larissa had fallen through.

"So…" Drew started out saying slowly, with his calm, well articulated voice. "I overheard Cameron talking to my mom. And I heard you're planning to take Larissa out to LA for a weekend."

I laughed. I couldn't contain the grin spreading across my face. So many of my friends didn't understand why I would do this. It was certainly a difficult concept for any normal person to wrap their mind around. "Yeah. It's going to be awesome." I told them with full confidence. I could tell they were insanely worried, but that didn't deter me from feeling as though this was exactly what I was supposed to do.

"Tom, you barely know this girl." Travis declared. "You were with her for three hours! Three hours, Tom! This is ridiculous! And that's coming from me!"

Travis was barely 21 and wasn't recognized for his wisdom. I had witnessed firsthand his history of bad decisions, and it was somewhat ironic for him to tell me something I was doing was stupid. That would have been a huge warning sign for any sensible person.

"Look," I replied with a mix of enthusiasm and defensiveness, unable to hide my grin. "This is an awesome idea. I can't fully explain to you why, but it just makes sense. I know this is what I'm supposed to do. Besides, LA is just a second home to me. We'll be hanging out with my friends, we'll certainly have separate sleeping arrangements, and it's just going to be a fun weekend. I don't see what your problem is with this."

The conversation carried on with us reasoning with each other. They still thought I was ridiculous, and I still thought I was awesome. They were still incredibly concerned but agreed not to say anything to Larissa, which was good enough for me. As long as nobody would screw this up, I'd be in excellent shape.

A few days later, I had plans to meet up with my friend Jared for pizza. He was about to get married and I wanted to touch base with him before then. His mom had expressed concern to me about the girl he was marrying, so I wanted to make sure he was making the right decision for himself. After we had finished talking about the relationship he had with his fiance, and the future they had ahead of them, I told him about this girl I had met and the date I would be taking her on. He had a very surprised laughter. Of course he thought I was crazy, just like anybody else that I talked to did.

"What are you going to do with her out there?" He asked.

I thought that was an odd way to word that question. "What am I going to *do with* her?" Not "What are *we* going to be doing while we're out there?"

I couldn't help but respond with the first sarcastic comment that popped into my head. "I'm going to slit her throat and dump her in the ocean." I said with an affirming voice. He almost looked slightly confused for only half a second before we simultaneously bursted into laughter.

"I'm just going to take her out to my favorite places, and we'll spend time with my friends. It'll just be a quick and fun weekend." I explained to him. Of course he had a difficult time grasping this concept like anybody with any amount of logic and reason would, be he was encouraging of my idea and wished the me the best, as I wished him all the best in his approaching marriage.

After several days of anticipation, it was finally time for Larissa to move into her apartment in Lancaster. I was finally going to see her again for the second time. After meeting with a prayer group for Young Life, Drew and I went to help her move in. After we finished taking her belongings from her car and mom's van to her room, we spent some time playing card games with her and her mother.

After a few games, it was beginning to get late. Mrs. Sutton decided to go to sleep and get rested before traveling back to New York the next day. Drew knew I was hoping to spend time alone with Larissa and decided to be a team player and not linger around. It was late, but Larissa was feeling very excited about her new home and the new city she was living in. We were feeling adventurous so we decided to go out and explore, since she lived right in downtown Lancaster City.

The city featured two buildings downtown that stood tall enough to stand out: one of which was a Marriott hotel, towering over the city with its 14 stories. We decided to go to the top and look out over the city.

We casually strolled into the fancy hotel in a "we're supposed to be here" kind of way and headed directly to the elevator. Unfortunately, the elevator only allowed us to go to the fourth floor without a room key. Once we entered onto the fourth floor, we walked to the stairwell and hiked the remaining 10 stories to the top floor. We opened the door and walked down the hall to the nearest window. We looked out of it only to find a view that wasn't anything overly impressive. Surely during the day you could see for miles, but the city of Lancaster didn't provide a vast amount of city lights to lighten up the night sky. Nothing like the endless lights of Los Angeles we would be seeing in a mere two weeks.

"You should see what it looks like overlooking LA." I told her with a big grin.

"Does it look much different than this?" She asked.

"Oh my goodness, yes! There's a hike at a park near Burbank that takes you to an incredible overlook where all you see is city lights three quarters of the way around you and they go on further than you can see." I told her. I did my best to subtly paint a picture that would make her wish she could go out there and see it for herself. She continued to ask questions about LA and I answered them with delight. I continued feeding her sub-conscious, doing my best to cause her to crave the opportunity to go there herself, and it was beginning to work.

After pointing out what I could in the horizon, we felt like we had seen all there was to see and walked back to the elevator, which fortunately didn't require a room key to go back down to the lobby. Once we were in the lobby, we decided to continue exploring what we could, walking down a hallway that was still under construction, restoring different historical parts of the building. It was mostly dark in that part of the building, so we just sat and talked. It felt so good to be around her again. Just like our constant texting, the conversation was easy. It was fun to just slow down for a moment and enjoy the conversation. It was already late, but we had to have been talking for over an hour. We talked about our families, our pasts, shared stories, and just talked about more random things than I could ever try and remember.

After we got tired of sitting, we decided to continue with our late night adventure. We walked to Steinman Park, which I wouldn't necessarily describe as a park, but it was more of a well-decorated area between two buildings. It had pretty lights, fountains and greenery: a very romantic location.

I knew I liked this girl, but I had fallen into these types of traps before. The trap of falling for someone and having them not fall back for you. "The friend zone" was something I was all too familiar with, and I was really hoping the same thing wouldn't happen with Larissa.

When I was barely out of high school, I had a friend named Christina. We were really close friends. Almost too close. We hung out constantly, but I wasn't trying to pursue any relationships at the time since I was focused on moving to LA and I didn't want anything or anyone holding me back. After a year of suppressing the feelings I had for her that were building up inside me I decided to make a move. It seemed beyond logical to start a relationship with someone that felt like your best friend. Not to mention, she seemed to really like me. A lot. I could only conclude she didn't openly share her feelings since she didn't want to hold me back from my ambitions in life. The thought of her selflessness made me all the more fond of her.

I eventually expressed my feelings to her only to find out she just wanted to be friends. All of the vibes, all of the hints, everything I thought was leading into something more had turned out to be nothing more than a misunderstood friendship. This tore me apart. At the time I had thought she was everything I wanted, and facing the rejection was tremendously difficult. Especially since I had felt led-on for such a long time. I tried to carry on our friendship as usual, but I eventually couldn't take it anymore. The feelings wouldn't go away and spending any time together only left me feeling more hurt and confusion. I needed to separate myself from feeling this way and work towards getting over her. The only option I felt I had was to cut her out of my life.

I numbingly cut off all communication ties with her whatsoever as my feelings of attraction had now twisted into feelings of loathing and resentment.

After about a month of not speaking with her, I contacted her so I could take her for a drive. I felt the end of our friendship at least needed some closure. I explained how I had felt led on for such a long time, and how I had been so strongly misled. I scolded her about how she needs to be more sensitive about the way she is towards guys. I told her exactly why I couldn't bring myself to be her friend anymore as she sat next to me in silence avoiding eye contact.

I have no idea if she was expecting me to apologize for how I suddenly shut her out as a friend, or if I would make an attempt to repair our broken friendship. I didn't have plans to do so. I drove several miles as I relentlessly vented to her about why I had harshly ended our friendship as she listened in painful silence. I drove back toward her home and dropped her off for the last time. "Have fun in LA." She said as she got out of my car, slamming the door behind her. I could tell she was fighting back tears as she walked back into her house. We parted our ways and I haven't heard from her since.

Whenever I look back and reflect on how I handled my friendship with Christina, I know there were more sensitive ways I could have, and probably should have, gone about it. My unfortunate purpose of that talk was not just to explain myself. I wanted revenge. I wanted to hurt her to the best of my ability after what she had put me through. Even though I felt hurt and misled, she certainly deserved better than for me to end our friendship the way I did.

From that point forward, whenever I became friends with a girl I took interest in, I would eventually be clear with them that I wanted to be more than just friends. Whenever I found myself to be categorized in "The Friend Zone", I cut them out of my life without a second thought and they wouldn't hear from me again. Last thing I needed was to be led on and I didn't feel the need to waste my time with friendships that wouldn't be leading into anything romantic. After all, I figured I wouldn't constantly be hanging out with other girls when I would eventually get married, and those friendships would eventually subside, anyway.

Larissa and I continued to talk and it seemed almost romantic as we were in such a beautiful setting. The moment seemed right, but I wanted to be cautious and guard my heart. I knew I liked this girl, and I thought she might like me back, but I've been proven wrong before.

I looked at her and said cautiously "Larissa, I need to be honest with you. I think you're really awesome. I really like you, but I've been severely misled in the past. I would like to know if there's any possibility we could get to know each other as more than friends."

She seemed almost surprised and a little terrified. Even though I thought it was blatantly obvious I had feelings for her, it seemed as though she did not see this coming. "Tom, you seem like a great guy and everything. I really appreciate you being upfront about this, but I *just* got out of a bad relationship, and I need to spend some time focusing on my relationship with God and try to find myself again."

My typical reaction to hearing this was to verbally respond as though just being friends was acceptable and follow it up with never speaking to her again, but I knew I needed to trust God more with my love life. Even though this girl seemed really great, I still wanted to embrace whatever life God had ahead of me, whether it was to be single for the rest of my life, or to eventually get married. I knew I needed to stop making irrational decisions based on the expectancy of getting married.

"It's alright" I responded to her with every bit of sincerity. The words coming out of my mouth felt completely unnatural, but I knew I needed to be trusting God in every aspect. "I don't care if I'm getting to know you as a friend, or as something more than that. I think you're really awesome and I genuinely want to continue getting to know you."

Even though the concept of maintaining a friendship that just might never mature into a relationship was a situation I had trained myself to avoid at all costs, I wanted to pour every bit of faith I had into the understanding that God had complete control over what He was doing in my life. I knew he had a purpose for introducing me to Larissa. If she was only going to be in my life as a friend, I wanted to trust in

God's purpose for bringing her into the picture, and embrace whatever life God had set out for me.

The previous attitude I held towards friendships with girls was not only selfish, but it was a reflection of the fact that I wasn't trusting in God's plan for my love life. My concern wasn't how to be a good friend or what I could contribute to a friendship, but I was primarily focused on what I could get out of the friendship, and where it was eventually going. I never had any concern about how my attitude would negatively affect the girls who I completely cut off without even saying "Goodbye".

Had I been trusting God with my love life, I would have not only been able to hold onto some incredible friendships, but I wouldn't have been so stressed. My stress was a direct result of my lack of trust in God's plan. The less I trusted in God with my love life, the more stress I was experiencing. I allowed that stress to ruin multiple friendships, which could have been salvaged had I been trusting in where God had me in life, and focusing on what He wanted to teach me.

I had finally reached a point where I could fully trust God in whatever direction my friendship with Larissa might go, but I still had a burning question I needed to ask. "So this weekend thing… Are we calling it a date or are we just going as friends?" I asked her cautiously as we proceeded back toward the car.

"It's going to have to be just as friends." She stated with confidence. "If you don't want to go anymore, I totally understand, but if we go, it can only be as friends."

"Yeah, it's totally cool. Friends it is. No worries!" I responded. Heck, even if we were just going as friends, I knew this was still going to be a lot of fun.

We got back into my trusty Subaru and headed back to drop her off at her apartment. After a few moments of silence, I looked at her and stated "You know, this city can only handle so much awesomeness, and sooner or later, we're going to have to join forces, or one of us is bound to become the villain."

She smiled and laughed then stated, "Well, I guess I'll just have to make sure I'm not the villain"

Even after I openly stated how I felt about her and she didn't reciprocate those feelings in any way, shape, or form, there was no sense of awkwardness as we were still enjoying our time hanging out. Our conversation and laughter came just as easily as it had before.

In the following two weeks before "this weekend thing" (as we referred to it), we spent a substantial amount of time together. It worked in my favor that she didn't know many people in the area, and I just so happened to be awesome. She would ride the tractor with me while I worked in the field, and sometimes even helped me milk the cows during the night shift--which typically went until 3AM. On several occasions, she came over and we watched movies together. Since she grew up in such a conservative household, I wanted to help catch her up on all the classics she'd missed out on: Zoolander, Happy Gilmore, and Monty Python and the Holy Grail just to name a few.

We were spending a lot of time together and it was beginning to almost feel like we were dating. Watching movies at my place was great, since my double-papasan chair was curved up around the edges like a giant nest naturally causing us to be seated closer together. I would sneak an arm around her during the movie and we would be sitting comfortably close.

After the movies ended, we would just stay up late talking about anything we had on our minds. We talked about our faith and began keeping each other spiritually accountable, sharing what God had been teaching us lately, and discussing what we were each learning from our devotions. We were still under the label of "friends" but I could feel it quickly becoming something much more.

As the day of our weekend trip approached, Larissa asked me what she should pack. I told her to bring some shorts, pants, t-shirts, bathing suit, jacket, snow goggles, a nice dress and heels, and of course, to be sure to be wearing a cardigan when we left. She seemed very confused by this list, as I intended, but she packed it all together. I had given her a couple things in the list to throw her off. Not that Los Angeles was anything close to where she expected we would be going.

Over the course of the next two weeks as the day of the trip approached, Drew would often urge me to tell her where we were going. His obsessive concern was really beginning to bother me. I really didn't want to spoil the surprise of a lifetime, but out of respect for Drew's serious concern, I did offer Larissa to tell her what the plan was for the weekend. She just smiled and declined my offer since she really loved surprises. I was perfectly okay with that.

The night before we left for the "weekend thing," I had to milk the cows until 3 a.m., followed by a Bible study and breakfast in the morning with my Young Life kids in the high school at 6:30. I knew this filled my entire night and morning, and I wouldn't have a chance to get any sleep the night before we left. I urged her to go home and get a full night's rest. After all, she would need it. She told me if I wasn't getting any sleep she wouldn't be either. She wanted to hang out with me while I worked, as she had done a handful of times up to this point.

As I was working, I received another text from Drew. "Tell her" he demanded. This was really starting to bother me. I couldn't understand why this had to be such a big deal to him and why he had so much concern over this when it had nothing to do with him.

I took a break from what I was doing in the barn and turned toward Larissa. "Look, Drew really wants me to tell you where we're going. And I just want to offer one last chance to tell you before we leave in the morning."

"I don't care what Drew thinks." She said "I don't know why it has to be of such concern to him. He said you were a good friend, so I don't know why he is acting like this. Besides I like surprises, and I know I can trust you, so I don't want to be told ahead of time where we're going."

"Alright, sounds good to me." I said with a smile. I was glad she enjoyed surprises, since I really enjoy surprising people. I didn't want to ruin a perfectly good surprise.

I finished the shift around 3:30 AM. My parents knew I would be taking her somewhere for the weekend and they said she could sleep on the couch while I went to campaigners. I got a shower so I could go to the high school without smelling like cow crap. When Larissa took her turn in the bathroom to shower and get cleaned up, I started packing my bags. She then came out dressed and ready, and helped me pack everything I needed into my bag by 5:30AM, just in time for me to prepare a few things and head to Campaigners. She was asleep on the couch by the time I left. I headed out to pick up a few of my guys and brought them to the high school.

Once Campaigners ended and school began, it was time to head back and get this adventure started. I swung by a flower shop and picked up a single rose for Larissa. This was still a "weekend thing" and we were going as "friends" but I figured things had progressed over the last couple weeks to the point that I felt she would appreciate being given a rose.

I headed back to my parents and woke her up. It was finally time to go. She only had a few hours of sleep, but she was excited to see what was ahead for the weekend. She was already dressed and ready to go with comfortable jeans and the cardigan, as I had recommended. We put our bags into the trunk of my car and I opened the door for her, revealing the rose sitting on her seat. She blushed a little as she smiled. "Thank you, I've never been given a single rose before!"

"You're welcome, I'm glad you like it." I said with a smile. "Are you ready to go?" I asked her in a tone that was more like I was asking her if she was ready for a challenge.

Her blush turned into more of a solid grin. "Let's go" she said as she sat down into her seat.

I started the car and our adventure began. Ahead of us lay an intense, life-changing weekend.

CHAPTER 4
The Dare

L arissa and I were in my car on the way to the airport. At this point we were simply two "friends" going on an adventure that could not be labeled as a "date". The drive felt long as my anticipation for the surprise continued to build. By now we had become quite comfortable with each other as friends. Our conversation flowed naturally as I drove further than she was expecting our adventure to take us. As we neared the airport, Larissa pointed out an airplane that was going in and out of the clouds. Little did she know, in a few hours, that was going to be us.

I nonchalantly took the exit for Dulles Airport as I hoped Larissa wouldn't notice any of the bold signs labeling where we were headed. Fortunately, she didn't think anything of it, since boarding an airplane was clearly the last thing on her mind. I pulled into a nearby Hilton Hotel, where I had reserved a place to park my car for the weekend. From there we would be taking the shuttle to the airport. As we pulled in, she looked at me with a slight amount of shock as if I had totally been misunderstanding her idea of friendship. I quickly raised my hand and explained. "Don't worry, we're not staying here!". The last thing I wanted was for her to think I was trying to get laid, and the last thing she wanted was for me to think she was that kind of girl. We were both devout Christians and fully committed to saving ourselves for marriage.

"Okay, good." She said, relieved. "What do you need here?" She asked.

"I just need to use the bathroom, and get a couple of things." I replied.

We went inside and used the restrooms. She walked back out as I was at the front desk getting my parking pass. I could feel Larissa staring through the back of my head as I spoke to the receptionist. The kind receptionist handed me my parking pass and gave me instructions on specifically where to park. I thanked her and walked back to Larissa.

"What was that about?" She asked looking very curiosity. I really had her confused now. Her mind had to have been all over the place trying to put the few pieces she had together. I held the paperwork with my left hand as she walked on my right out of the hotel and back towards the car. I could tell her eyes were wandering toward the paper as it swung back and forth with my hand as I walked.

"I'll tell you in a minute." I said as I looked at her with a smile.

We got in the car and I moved it to the back of the lot under some trees. I turned off the engine as I placed the parking pass in the windshield. I stepped out and walked over to the passenger side as she stood up, preparing myself to tell her the last thing she would ever expect to hear.

"Ok, here's what we're going to do." I started off speaking confidently in a matter-of-fact kind of way. "We are going to get on a shuttle, take that shuttle to the airport, and we're going to get on an airplane and fly to Los Angeles for the weekend." I said, firing off the list without skipping a beat.

Larissa laughed as if I had just made a joke, clearly disbelieving there was any truth to what I had just told her. "You're lying to me." She said in a nervous laugh. "Tell me what's really going on." Her eyes were wide open in disbelief.

"It's true. I'm being totally serious." I said to her trying to be casual while trying not to smile too hard. "I brought you a small suitcase to pack your stuff into to use as a carry-on, and small bottles for all your liquids so we don't have any trouble getting through security. I have separate sleeping arrangements planned at my friend's place for both nights. If you're not comfortable staying with my friends, I'll be happy to pay for your own hotel room. On Sunday night we'll be taking a red-eye flight back and we'll be home Monday morning." I held up the papers I had been holding in my hand so she could see what they were and remove any remaining doubt. "Here's our airline tickets, and the reservation for the rental car."

A large smile started to spread over her face as she realized that I wasn't kidding and this was actually happening. I continued explaining what the plan was as she was coming to terms of this crazy reality. "Once you re-pack everything we'll grab the next shuttle and head to the airport. We've got about two and a half hours until our flight leaves, so that puts us in pretty good shape"

"Alright" She said with an enormous smile as she slowly nodded her head. "Let's go for it!" She headed towards the trunk of the car to started repacking what she needed. I stepped away and and walked over to the drivers side to give her some privacy. Larissa was quickly moving her belongings over to the small suitcase, leaving behind anything she felt wasn't necessary.

As soon as she was finished packing, I approached her with a burning question. Obviously our friendship had progressed in the past two weeks, and I couldn't help but try one more time to add some kind of a label to this trip. "So... are we going to call this our first date?" I asked softly, and cautiously.

Surely now that she knew where we were going, hopefully she would realize how awesome it would be to call it a date. With how well things had been going for us as friends, and given how well she reacted to the game plan for the weekend, I felt the odds were pretty great she would be comfortable with calling this a date. And besides, calling this our "first date" would certainly put all other first dates to shame.

She looked toward me and nodded with a shy smile. "Yes, we can call this our first date."

Mission accomplished. This was going to be my first date in probably two years, and I was lucky enough to land this date with "The most awesomest thing God put on the planet."

We pulled our bags out of the trunk and locked the car once we were confident we had everything we needed. We walked towards the hotel entrance to wait for the next shuttle. "So were you surprised?" I asked her. Of course I knew she was surprised. I just wanted to hear her say so.

Larissa was still smiling from ear to ear as she was still coming to terms with the reality of everything that had come together so quickly. "Yes, I was surprised. This was very... spontaneous." She said as she smiled in a way that made me feel like I couldn't have come up with a better idea for our first date. The date may have seemed spontaneous to her, but I had this planned for five weeks.

I was relieved Larissa was agreeing to this date so willingly. I was prepared with what I would say if she had any hesitation. "Don't let me out-awesome you" would have been the first thing I would have said to her. I know she wouldn't let me get away with being more awesome, or being too intense for her. "Do you remember when Aladdin stood on the magic carpet with his hand fully extended asking Jasmine if she trusted him?" I was prepared to ask. "She would have missed out on A Whole New World!" There was no way she would have backed down after I laid down such an accurate pun/Aladdin reference, no matter how corny it was. Worst case scenario, I would hand over the keys to my car, fly to LA by myself, and have a full weekend to rethink my approach.

Fortunately, Larissa was 100% on board and I didn't have to lay down either card. The shuttle arrived and we climbed on board. Within 15 minutes we arrived at the airport with plenty of time to spare. We went to a kiosk and printed out our tickets. Going through security was effortless, even though she was worried about her ticket that said "Larissa Godfrey-Sutton" instead of "Larissa Sutton" as it stated on her driver's license. I bought the tickets and filled out her name to match the way it was listed on her Facebook profile. I could only assume it was her legal name. After all, when I bought the tickets, I'd known her for only five days.

We arrived at our terminal and had plenty of time to spare before departure. I bought Auntie Anne's pretzels for us to share while we talked and waited for our flight. By this time Larissa had come to grips with the reality that we would be in LA for the weekend. We talked about the different things we could do and see while we were there. I had a light agenda, but I wanted to stay open to any ideas she had in case there was anything specific she wanted to see. I was feeling relieved this crazy idea didn't fall through. All my planning and absurd confidence in the gut feeling God gave me had paid off.

Finally, our plane arrived and it was time to get on board. We found our seats and settled in for our 5 hour flight. I had brought a headphone splitter so we could listen to music together. I had assembled a playlist that morning for us to listen to. The first song on the list was "Chasing Cars" by Snow Patrol. The lyrics of the song seemed to fit us perfectly in the moment. It felt as if we were on our way to "a garden that's bursting into life." This was a pretty serious adventure like neither of us had experienced. For me, Los Angeles was just visiting my second home, but being able to take this incredible girl there and share it with made it truly exciting. For her, she was suddenly going to a place she had always wanted to visit without any prior knowledge of the trip. And of course, being able to experience it with a guy as awesome as me, was really lucky on her part.

We continued listening to the playlist I had made, mouthing the words as if we were singing at the top of our lungs. I'm sure the guy sitting next to us thought we were totally crazy, but we were both having too much fun to care.

The flight took off in the late evening and our airplane was flying directly into the sunset, which caused this to be the longest sunset of my life. Our five hour non-stop flight didn't seem to take very long at all since Larissa and I kept ourselves so well entertained.

Meanwhile, my family was at home eating lunch. My parents were under the assumption I had taken Larissa to New

York to visit her family, since I wouldn't tell them and they were left to guess as to where we were headed. My mom had asked Larissa where we were going, only for her to respond with "Wait, you don't know either?!".

Since I had been so secretive about the plan, they asked my brother, Sam, if I had told him where I was taking Larissa for the weekend. Sam was the only one in my family I had told where I would be taking her.

"Tom took Larissa to Los Angeles." He replied, as he knew there was no surprise to spoil for anyone by this time.

My dad couldn't help himself but to sigh with a little bit of a laugh. "Sounds like something Tom would do." My parents knew how crazy and spontaneous I could be. Taking things to the next level had always come naturally. Even though this was a wild concept, it was well within the realm of things I was capable of.

Back on the plane, Larissa and I were having fun taking selfies, telling stories, and planning out our weekend. The flight began descending towards LAX as we fastened our seatbelts and prepared for the landing. Once the flight had landed and parked at our terminal, we grabbed our bags and headed toward the door. We made our way up the aisle of the plane, making slow progress, as the long line of people ahead of us started moving. "Get ready" I said, turning back to Larissa as I walked. "Start dreaming!"

"Dreaming about what?" She gave me a puzzled look as I gave her these odd instructions as we approached the door of the plane.

"Just start dreaming about something!" I told her as if it was the most important thing she would do all day. As soon as she got to the door I exclaimed "Get ready... and HOP!!" She hopped off the plane into the jetway, still confused about my instructions, but still had a huge smile on her face as she laughed at what she didn't realize was a huge setup.

"HA!!!" I said loudly while pointing at her "You just hopped off a plane at LAX with a dream and a cardigan!" Of course, this was a direct reference to the song "Party In The USA" by Miley Cyrus, which was wildly popular just a few years earlier.

She began laughing. "That's the reason you wanted me to wear a cardigan?"

"Totally worth it, right?" I asked her while I grinned at my clever joke. That was the only reason I told her to wear a cardigan, and she did. I was sure she thought it was funny and totally lame at the same time, but was totally worth it.

We stepped outside and grabbed the shuttle that would take us to the rental cars. As soon as we picked up the car I had reserved, we headed straight for In-N-Out, the restaurant she had unknowingly agreed to allow me to take her to. I ordered a double-double and she ordered a cheeseburger. We prayed over our meal thanking God for our safe trip and the awesome adventure we were on.

I sank my teeth into the burger. Oh, how I missed this burger. They were so good, and unfortunately only available in the south-west. Larissa enjoyed her burger but not as much as I did. An In-N-Out Burger love affair is something that grows over time.

We finished our meal and drove a couple miles to Playa Del Rey, where my friend Dave lived. Before going to his apartment, I parked near the beach so we could take a walk by the ocean. It was dark and cold, but light of the night sky was just bright enough for us to see. This was her first time walking on a beach of the pacific ocean. We enjoyed the sounds of the waves crashing and the blowing wind was making her cold so I shared my coat with her.

The entire flight I was contemplating if I should be so bold as to ask her to be my girlfriend, and how I would do so. After all, this was originally supposed to be a trip "as friends", and I gracefully broke through that barrier. As we stood there at the ocean hugging each-other, doing our best to stay warm, the moment felt right, and I couldn't pass it up. I had to trust my gut instinct on this one, too.

"What's the craziest thing you've ever done?" I asked.

"Uh, a spontaneous trip to California" she said with a slight laugh as though it was obvious that this date was certainly it.

"Mind if I dare you to do something crazier?" I said with a little bit of a smile, yet challenging her for the next crazy thing.

"What could that be?" She asked looking out toward the ocean as if the answer lay among the crashing waves. Surely I couldn't possibly dare her to do anything crazier than fly to California for a weekend. That would be too difficult to top.

"I dare you to be my girlfriend" I challenged her as I smiled into her face. I had to make sure I sounded serious enough so she wouldn't think I was kidding.

After a brief pause she looked at me and smirked.

"And what's the penalty if I say no?" She said with a curious smile. To her, any dare has to have a penalty if you object.

I didn't plan for this response. I couldn't help but give her the most sarcastic response that popped into my head. "I'll slit your throat and dump you into the ocean." I said looking at her attempting to look serious, but not serious enough to think I wasn't joking.

We erupted into laughter. Of course she knew I was just making a joke. At least I'm pretty sure she did.

"Well, in that case...Sure, I'll take you up on your dare." She said with a smile. "I'll be your girlfriend."

Another Mission accomplished. I was currently holding the most awesome girl in the world in my arms, and she was now my girlfriend. I held her hand and had a huge smile on our faces as we walked back to the car.

Before the night was getting too late, we needed to head to my friend Dave's apartment, which was only two blocks away. Dave was a guy I had met while rock climbing in Malibu. We climbed together almost every week when I lived in California, and every time I visited after moving back to PA.

When we arrived at his apartment, he was happy to let us in. He had just had his wisdom teeth pulled and was feeling somewhat out of it. His mouth was swollen so it wasn't easy for him to talk. Even though he was low on energy and enthusiasm, it was still great to see him. I introduced Larissa as my girlfriend for the first time. Even though talking wasn't too easy for him, we were able to catch up and enjoy our time visiting.

It was already late by the time Larissa and I had gotten there, and after we spent some time catching up, it was nearing midnight. I hadn't had any sleep the night before and were were still on Pennsylvania time, which made it even worse. Larissa slept in the spare bedroom and I slept on the leather couch. The next morning we said goodbye to Dave and grabbed breakfast at iHop. We lightly discussed the plan for the day as we ate, and our goal was to pack as much into the weekend we could.

Our first stop was Point Dume. The drive there from where we were in Playa Del Rey would primarily consist of driving up Route 1, also known as the Pacific Coastal Highway. This particular highway goes up the entire west coast with beautiful views of the ocean, jutted rocks, and mountains. We set off for the PCH after breakfast and even though the sky was overcast. Larissa seemed to enjoy the beautiful views, although she seemed even more impressed with the Lamborghinis and Ferraris driving by us. I have no idea what the occasion was, but we saw more exotic cars that day than I had ever seen in the entire year while I lived there.

After a beautiful drive, we arrived at Point Dume and walked across the beach towards the beautiful rock face. This was still my favorite place on earth. I pointed out the bolts on the cliff for rock climbing. Several fond memories of climbing there were rushing back to me as I pointed out the different routes leading up the face of the cliff. There was nothing like stepping out of the sand right onto a rock face. It was the best of both worlds. I walked her around to the other part of the cliff, which featured my favorite route in the world, "The West Face." This particular route was around the corner with my back to the ocean. It was an awesome challenging route with amazing views of the ocean, the beach, and several tourists gawking in amazement.

Larissa and I hiked up a trail that took us up and around to the top of Point Dume where we could overlook the legendary Malibu Beach and Pacific Ocean. As we reached the top of the trail on the mainland and headed out onto the top of the rock. We saw a man holding his two year old child and a dog was following him. He looked strangely familiar. I was sure I recognized him from somewhere. After a brief moment, it clicked. I realized why I had recognized him from, but this couldn't seriously be true. I thought for sure it was him, but I needed a second opinion. I whispered to Larissa "Is that-"

"Mhmmm!" She nodded wide-eyed in amazement. "That's Owen Wilson." We were both taken aback by this random, but fortunate encounter.

"Hey Owen" I said casually, "mind if we get a picture with you?"

"No, no pictures." He said in a kind and soft tone as if he were asking a favor of us, not rudely rejecting us. Of course I took the wrong approach. Besides, he's out with his kid. He just wants to spend time out of the spotlight and enjoy this beautiful day. I suddenly felt like I had been somewhat rude for even asking him. He does deserve to have personal time. Looking back, I should have pretended I didn't know who he was and asked him to take a picture of me and Larissa. If I treated him like a normal human being, maybe he would have been interested in a conversation. (I'm going to keep that idea in mind next time I bump into somebody famous.)

"Holy crap, that was Owen Wilson!" Larissa and I said to each other almost simultaneously in a slightly above whisper tone of voice. He was already on his way down the trail towards the beach. We couldn't believe we just had a brief run-in with one of the most famous people in Hollywood.

Larissa and I walked the the end of the trail for Point Dume, which was a sheer cliff that dropped off, where you could see large boulders 60 feet below you on the shore right before it turned into ocean. Looking northward you could see the beach and all the people down below. Most of the fog had lifted and It was a turning into a beautiful day, and the view was as breathtaking, as always. This particular place contained everything I love about California.

We hiked back down to the beach and continued on with our adventurous day. We got back into the car and headed towards Route 1. As we exited the beach parking, I noticed Owen Wilson walking along the parking lot. I rolled down my driver's side window with the intent to say something respectfully to him without being a bother. "Have a good day, Mr. Wilson." I said with a kind smile and a small wave.

"Thanks, you too." He said with some enthusiasm in his soft voice as he gave us a gentle smile. He sounded genuine, too. It would have been great to have the opportunity to talk with him and get to know him more, but I wanted to respect his privacy. I'm sure he has strangers like me approaching him often enough.

The next stop for me and Larissa was the Ferrari dealership in Malibu. Of course, I hadn't told her that was where we were going. I wanted to fit in any surprise I could. When I drove past the dealership to park on the street her eyes were glued on the cars right outside her window. I parked the car and we walked inside. We wandered around and looked closely at all the gorgeous works of art. The showroom also contained Maserati's and high end Porsche's. We both dreamed of owning a car like one of these someday. We still do.

After getting our fill of dream cars we couldn't afford, we made a swift exit and drove down the street to another dealership that had some Lamborghinis in their showroom. That was more of Larissa's style. We stood and gawked at them, taking pictures and standing in admiration of the loads of horsepower surrounding us.

We would have loved to stay longer, but it was time for our next stop. After all, there were several things to see in California and we only had two days. Each stop was an express adventure and I aimed to keep this first date as intense and interesting as possible.

Larissa bid farewell to her dream cars as we got back into our not-so-fascinating rental car. I drove us to Malibu Creek where I had logged several hours of rock climbing in the time I had lived there. This was another one of my favorite places I was really eager to share with her.

After I parked the car it was about a mile long hike to the swimming hole which was the gateway to the rock climbing area in the park. I grabbed the climbing shoes we had brought and we started walking. On the hike in, you'd never expect there to be a place to actually swim. The creek was mostly dried up, and the path we walked on looked as if it hadn't seen rain in years. Once we got to the swimming hole, there were a few groups of people doing some cliff jumping into the water. It sure looked like fun, but we weren't prepared to swim, we were there to climb.

A couple weeks prior, I had told my buddy Scott Lunsford I would be taking a girl out to Cali and we'd like to do some climbing. Scott was another guy I had done a lot of climbing with while I was living out there. He routinely climbed incredibly difficult routes, and his muscles were incredibly tone, enabling him to do so. I had told him I wouldn't have much time for climbing, but if he was able to do some climbing on this particular day with a friend, Larissa and I would be able to join them for a route or two.

Getting to the climbing was always a fun challenge. The swimming hole acted as an obstacle and we had to traverse the rocks on the left side above the water to get back to the climbing areas. I helped Larissa traverse the rock to make sure she wouldn't fall in the water. Getting to the climbing section known as Mt. Gorgeous, where we would find Scott, involved some maneuvering which would almost be considered climbing in itself. It also involved a brief hike up a steep hill which could easily tire any ordinary person.

When we arrived to the location where Scott was, he greeted me with great enthusiasm and a strong handshake. His friend, Sebastian Roche greeted me warmly as well. I had climbed with Sebastian on a previous occasion, so he was relatively familiar to me. Sebastian was a successful actor. At the time he was back from New York taking a break from filming "A Walk Among the Tombstones" with Liam Neeson. I had seen him in a few other TV shows including Criminal Minds and Fringe. Larissa hadn't caught onto the fact that he was a TV star until after our return, only to realize he starred in one of her favorite TV shows. To which she did freak out and kick herself for not realizing it when she met him.

So after a few minutes of catching up, it was time to climb. "How much experience does she have? Think we should put her on this 5.10?" Scott asked me.

"I think she should be able to handle it" I told him. "She's pretty intense."

I'm not sure why I had so much faith in her rock climbing abilities. After all, a 5.10 is on the more difficult side of intermediate climbs. I had been climbing more difficult routes than that for years, and I was not very good at putting myself in the shoes of beginners.

Larissa didn't know what I was putting her up to as she innocently slipped her harness and shoes on while I got on belay and tied her in. She started up the wall. The first half of the climb wasn't too difficult and she pulled it off quite well. As the climb became more inverted she began having difficulty. Her progress slowed and it seemed she was almost stuck at one particular spot only about ten feet from the top. She clung to the rocks holding on for dear life.

"Tom! I have to tell you something!!" Larissa yelled down in exhaustion. "I'm not intense!!" I had officially pushed her too hard.

I shouted her some instructions to the best of my ability. Meanwhile Scott was getting roped into the route beside her. He climbed right on up like a spider and got to where she was in no time. He pointed out the places to put her feet and hands. Gave her some encouraging words, which then challenged her to push herself to finish the route, since she would feel much more accomplished than if she were to turn back.

Larissa managed to continue on with the climb and reach the top. She leaned back on the rope and I belayed her safely back to the ground. She was beyond exhausted. Considering it was her first time climbing, she burned her arms out on the climb rather than shifting most of her body weight down to her feet. This is a mistake I see happen with new climbers all the time. However, putting her on an easier route and giving her a few pointers would have been a good idea. She sat down and relaxed while I got tied in to do a route. It was a 5.11 with decent holds, but severely inverted. This one would be good since it would make me look all the more impressive to my new girlfriend, which, of course, was incredibly important.

This route was one of the more challenging routes I was able to climb. I worked my way up using a lot of brute strength, as you have to on any route that is hung back. I fell once on my way up, but managed to get back on and keep going. I reached the top feeling awesome and accomplished. Scott lowered me to the ground and congratulated me on such an excellent climb. He was always very encouraging and challenged me to push myself.

When I looked at the time, I knew we needed to get going. The unfortunate part of packing so much into a single weekend is how little time there is for everything you want to do. I had plans for us to be at Natalie and Michelle's house in 45 minutes. Natalie and Michelle were twins that I had become friends with when I moved to California. We had plans to join our friend Allyson and go to Santa Monica for dinner and celebrate their friend's birthday. Since the plan was to have a formal dinner at a nice restaurant, I was sure to pack my suit, and I made sure Larissa packed a dress and heels.

We said goodbye to Scott and Sebastian as we headed out of Malibu creek. We climbed down the boulders known as "The Stumbling Blocks", and traversed back across the water before making it back to the trail. We held hands as we walked along the dry path back to the car talking about the climbing we had just done.

After we finished our long hike, we got back into the car and drove to Burbank so we could meet up at Natalie and Michelle's house. We knocked on the door and were immediately welcomed in. I introduced Larissa to Natalie, Michelle, and Allyson. It was great to see them again, and they were asking Larissa all kinds of questions about this crazy adventure I had brought her on. They knew I had an audacious, risk-taking personality, but this was still off the charts for what they were used to. Of course they thought I was crazy when I told them ahead of time I would be taking this girl to LA for a date, but they were always supportive of my ideas, no matter how absurd they might be.

The girls were very welcoming to Larissa, as I knew they would be. They laughed as Larissa humored them with stories from the adventure we had up to that point. While they were busy getting along, I went to a nearby room and changed into my suit. I made sure to dress to impress. I had my full suit, along with my black vest and black tie. I looked good. Larissa was still having fun while getting to know the others by the time I came back out. She then dipped out of the conversation to get into her dress. Meanwhile I had the opportunity catch up with my friends. They were loaded with questions about how I met Larissa, and what had prompted me to take her on such a crazy date. They laughed about how this had topped any of the numerous crazy things I had done when I lived out there.

Once Larissa was dressed and ready to go, we all climbed into the rental car and headed to Santa Monica so we could rendezvous with their friends. When we arrived, we were surrounded by palm trees and beautiful ocean views. I found a convenient parking spot and I walked Larissa and my friends to the restaurant. We stepped inside to find out how classy, and upscale this place was.

The party of friends were waiting for us at a table in a separate room. Larissa and I took a seat as Natalie, Michelle, and Allyson introduced us to them. Larissa and I glanced over the menu only to find out the prices were steep. Sure, for our first date I had already paid for two airline tickets, and a rental car, but the idea of spending $45 on a single plate didn't come across as a logical expense. Besides, when I'm in California, any time I'm eating anything that isn't In-N-Out, is a wasted opportunity. Larissa was only hungry enough for a side salad, while I ordered a grilled cheese sandwich and tomato soup, which set me back a ridiculous $12. The upsetting part, in my mind, was that I could have had three double doubles and a drink for less than that and it would have filled me up.

After the meal, the girls were planning to go out dancing, but I was developing a migraine. Larissa and I walked out to the Santa Monica Pier so I could avoid the loud music. It was dark, but the pier was well lit, making our walk all the more cozy. The ocean air was mildly cold, so I handed Larissa my suit jacket so she could keep warm. We took a walk down to the beach, where the light from the pier and it's landmark ferris wheel enabled us to see pretty well as we walked through the sand.

We continued walking around making our best attempt to stay warm as my headache continued to worsen. Larissa had sore feet from her heels, and my feet were hurting from my uncomfortable shoes as well. After we spent a couple of hours at the beach, making the best of our time together, we walked back to where we parked the car. By the time we got there, we were both feeling relatively miserable. We had done a lot of walking, our feet hurt, my head hurt, it was late, and we were tired from our lack of sleep. It certainly put a damper on the evening. Not too long afterwards, the girls met up with us and I drove everyone back to Natalie and Michelle's. From there Allyson drove home. The twins had a spare bed for me to sleep in and a floor mattress in their room for Larissa.

I was hoping to go to my old church the next morning, but since our evening went so late, and my need to recover from a brutal headache, I wanted to get the sleep I needed in order to recover before starting the next day. When I crawled out of bed, Larissa and the girls were already eating breakfast downstairs. I joined them for the meal and asked if either Natalie or Michelle were able to join us for any sightseeing during the day. Unfortunately, they were both heading back to school and wouldn't have time. After we finished eating, we grabbed our bags and said farewell to my friends as we packed back into the car.

I decided the best way to take advantage of our last day there was to take Larissa to some of the most iconic places in Los Angeles. Our first stop was Hollywood Boulevard. To me it had lost it's appeal, but I felt the famous landmark was certainly worth taking her to see. We decided to look for Julia Robert's star, since she looked so much like her (I wasn't the only person to think so, either). I figured it would be neat for her to get a picture with it. After searching endlessly without any luck, I called my brother, Sam, and asked if he could look it up on the internet for me. Smartphones were, for the most part, mainstream, but I was in no rush to get one. Sam looked it up while I was on the phone with him only to discover that Julia Roberts didn't have a star, which I though was rather surprising. As Larissa and I explored the Walk of Fame, she was impressed with all the famous names written on the stars in the sidewalk. I walked her over to where we could see the Hollywood sign. It was far in the distance, but it was there. And of course, you can't go to Hollywood without seeing the Hollywood sign. We then headed back to the car for our next stop: City Walk.

City Walk is a beautiful collection of stores, restaurants, and street performers right outside of Universal Studios. There's enough entertainment to satisfy any individual who doesn't want to spend the money to go inside the widely recognized theme park. Larissa was mesmerized by the beautiful fountains, palm trees, as well as the beautifully featured brand-name stores and famous restaurants throughout the open air shopping center. We stopped to watch the indoor skydiving at iFly, which features a clear, vertical wind tunnel strong enough to keep a person suspended in the air. We then walked into a few of the shops, many of them featuring several souvenirs, candies, clothes and more. I bought her a purple sweatshirt that said Hollywood in bright white letters so she could have something physical to remind her of our date. We treated ourselves to some deliciously healthy smoothies at Jamba Juice after we spent plenty of time wandering around, taking in the amazing sights.

Before we would be heading to the airport that evening to catch our red-eye flight, there was one more stop I wanted to make. I wanted to take her to the town I used to live in: Sierra Madre.

Sierra Madre is what I would describe as LA's best kept secret. It's a small town just east of the well recognized city of Pasadena. It's so small, people who have lived in southern California for years haven't even heard of it. When I lived in this town, I felt completely removed from the intimidating hustle and bustle of the city. It's a town that feels so small you almost forget you're in the county of Los Angeles. There are no stop lights, just numerous four-way stop signs. A blind person could safely wander around the town, as people drive respectably slow and make sure they stop for any person that looks as though they might be walking across. The police force has nearly thirty cops on their force to patrol the square mile and a half that was nestled comfortably against the San Gabriel Mountains.

We arrived in the quaint town, passing under the beautiful trees and driving by the beautiful homes. I took Larissa directly to the town's signature coffee shop, Bean Town, which is located in the center of the town. I bought her a coffee and we sat down and relaxed on an old sofa, which was placed in the center of the shop. We took a moment to slow down and reflect upon our crazy weekend, which was quickly coming to an end. We sat there just soaking in the peaceful vibes of Sierra Madre. I don't know if everyone that visits this town gets such an overwhelming sense of peace when they visit, but I know I certainly do. The only understanding I have is that this town feels like home. It feels like that's where I belong, and that's where I'm supposed to be. Larissa was loving the town and catching all the same vibes.

Right beside us a man was doing a pastel and water-color painting. We struck up a conversation with him as we observed his beautiful work. When he found out we were in California for such a short time for our first date, he was inspired by our sense of adventure. He assured us that we must have great things in store for our future. He gave us a couple of his paintings to take home with us, and he wished us well in our newfound relationship.

We walked outside to the town square and decided to walk up the street to where I used to live. It was long, but it was nice to walk by all the beautiful houses with the exotic plants and trees. Walking around the town was also lovely, simply because it felt so quaint.

Once we reached the top of the hill, we arrived at my old home. 5 West Carter Avenue. It was an older home, with front steps that resembled an Aztec Temple. The house was so old, but had so much personality. When I lived there, I had three roommates. All three guys were at least five years older than I was, and enrolled in grad school. Even though there was a slight disconnect in education and maturity levels, we still had plenty of competitive fun with Mario Kart on the Wii, evening games of Settlers of Catan, and the occasional poker tournament. Seeing the house again brought back several happy memories of the time I lived there.

We hiked back down the hill and got to the car. I drove her up to the top of the hill onto a new road which lead past my old house, winding upward into the mountain. The end of the road brought us to an area that was under development. This area was being developed when I lived there, but still didn't have any sign of construction beginning for new houses to be built. This new road wound around to the top of the hill where it overlooked LA. At the end of the road we parked and got out to a plot of land that was level, just waiting for a house to be built. When I lived there I dreamed of being able to build a house right where my feet were planted. Since there still wasn't a house, I presented it to Larissa as the perfect place to build a home. She admired the view of city lights as it overlooked not just Sierra Madre, but the entire San Gabriel Valley. The incredible view was partially blocked by the cloud, since it had become overcast, chilly, and it had begun to drizzle.

Meanwhile, I was keeping an eye on the time. The remainder of our date was quickly coming to an end, so we took advantage of every minute we had. After enjoying our time at this overlook for several minutes, it was time to go home. We loathed the idea of leaving, but we promised ourselves we would return again soon. We got back into the car and headed for the airport. Before returning the car, we swung by to see Dave one last time. I knocked on the door and he opened it inviting us in. I thanked him for giving us a place to crash and told him I hoped we would see him again soon.

From there, Larissa and I headed to the return the rental car. I soon realized I had less than ideal time for everything I needed to do. Our flight would be taking off in 45 minutes. Sure, I had in mind how efficient the airport was, but there was something I hadn't put into consideration: Returning the rental car.

As I pulled into the lot, I drove over the directional spikes that will pop your tires if you try to leave the lot. Larissa's eyes got incredibly wide as she clenched her teeth and covered her face with her hands. She was convinced we were about to have a four tire blowout. I laughed at her reaction as I drove over them without any hesitation. I parked the car and we grabbed our luggage. I went to the counter to hand over the keys and receive my receipts only to watch the shuttle leave the station. The next shuttle to the airport would be in another 20 minutes. Putting us down to a very uncool time of 25 minutes to get to our plane by the time it arrived. We did our best to wait patiently as our hearts nervously pounded. After what felt like hours, it finally arrived.

We were not in a very good situation. We sat anxiously while the shuttle casually waited for more people. Finally after a few minutes, it closed it's doors and we were on our way. We arrived at the airport and the shuttle made a stop at Terminal 1. Then Terminal 2. Time was flying by as the shuttle continued to make slow progress. My heart felt as though it was pounding out of my chest. I had never missed a flight before. I didn't even know what happens when you miss a flight. This wasn't the ideal time to find out, either. Finally the shuttle made a stop at our terminal. We stepped off the bus with 11 minutes until our flight was scheduled for departure.

We ran to the desk and presented our ID's for the lady to print off our tickets. She looked closely at them. "I'm sorry, Miss. I can't let you on the plane with your ID. You'll never get past security. Your ticket is under Larissa Godfrey-Sutton, but your ID says Larissa Sutton."

I was in the ultimate state of urgency. "We didn't have a problem with it when we flew here. We'll do just fine!" I said forcefully.

"Well you're never going to make it to your flight in time. You only have ten minutes to get through security." She said confidently.

"Don't doubt us. We can make it!" I said back. At this point I was desperate and I wasn't going to allow these petty things to stop us from getting on this flight.

She seemed to be taking all the time in the world as if there was no rush. "Fine then. Here you go." She said. I'm sure she was hoping we'd miss our flight.

We ran off toward security as fast as we could. Or at least in the direction we thought was security. We soon realized we went the wrong way. We ran back, past the lady at the desk, awkwardly smiling and waving as we ran. We turned the corner and went up the stairs to find a line of people waiting to go through security. We stood there for a minute. I knew there was no way we were going to make it in time waiting in this line. It wasn't an option if we wanted to get on the plane. We excused ourselves through the line of people, while being as apologetic as we could. People didn't seem to be angry with us. I'm sure they could asuum we were running late, reading the desperation on our faces.

We got to the security guard that checks ID's and tickets. He didn't even say anything about the "Godfrey-Sutton" predicament. He was kind enough to unhook a rope for us to go through straight to the security and bypass the rest of the line of people. Proceeding through the metal detectors went flawlessly, only to find the security guards casually searching through my backpack. Since I forgot to empty my water bottle, they needed to confiscate it and thoroughly check my bag. My heart was pounding in my chest as the possibility of missing our flight became more and more realistic. After what felt like eternity, they handed me my backpack. Larissa waited to the side as I grabbed my belongings and we ran to the gate at the end of the terminal in our socks, with our belts over shoulders, and our shoes in our hands.

"Don't worry, you made it!" The man at the gate said as soon as we arrived. He could tell we wcrc in a huge sense of panic.

We both sighed with relief. I handed him our tickets as we put our shoes and belts on. He scanned our tickets and handed them back to us. "Have a nice flight." He said with a reassuring smile.

We walked down the jetway and stepped onto the plane. As soon as we took our first step into the plane, they fastened the door shut behind us. Larissa and I looked at our tickets only to find we had been given separate seats. Not cool, but at least we were on the plane. We said goodbye and headed to our seats. I sat down and reflected on the past weekend. I shut my eyes and did my best to sleep until we arrived at Dulles in the morning. We were going home.

CHAPTER 5
Interrogations

I t was 8AM when we arrived at Dulles airport. I held Larissa's hand as we walked towards where our shuttle would be picking us up. We sat on the bench, exhausted. Sleeping on a flight is never easy, and being an overnight flight, neither of us felt we got the rest we needed.

We waited for what seemed like an eternity. We laughed as we reflected on our crazy weekend. It almost seemed like a surreal dream. Finally, the shuttle arrived and we climbed on board. When we safely arrived back at my car, we threw our luggage into the trunk and started driving home.

We were about halfway home when my phone rang. It was my mom. I had Larissa answer since I was driving. "Hello?" Larissa answered, as she knew this could potentially be an awkward conversation.

"So, am I talking to a friend, a girlfriend, a fiance, or a wife?" I overheard my mom say while Larissa held the phone to her ear.

"Well, I'm certainly not a wife or a fiance, but I am a girl-friend." She responded with an awkward laugh.

The conversation continued awkwardly for a few minutes as my mom had so many questions. "Your mom wants to know when we'll be back" Larissa whispered.

"Let her know we'll be back in time for lunch." I said confidently. We still had an hour of driving until we would be home.

Upon our arrival at my parent's house for lunch, we were greeted warmly. We joined them at the dinner table and they had us share the story of our first date. The family laughed as they heard the details. Larissa, in her typical storytelling fashion, gave them all the works, using sound effects, facial expressions, and hand gestures to describe the chain of events, as well as her reaction from her point of view. She was very enthusiastic and energetic as she shared our story. It was a lot more fun listening to her than to try and explain it myself.

Since we were home, and now a few solid days into our relationship, I brought it to Larissa's attention that we needed to make our relationship Facebook official. Before we made any updates, she wanted to tell her family directly, so they didn't have to find out through social media.

Larissa's family is very conservative. The easiest way for me to explain exactly how conservative they are would be to say they were raised somewhere between Mennonite and Amish on the conservative scale. The girls were raised to wear dresses and head coverings. They helped with work in the kitchen and chores around the house. They had a TV, but they weren't allowed to watch it very often.

At this point, not all her siblings were still as conserva-tive, but most of them had grown in their Christian faith.

Her family consisted of eight children. Five girls and three boys. She began making phone calls, managing to reach only a few of them, and leaving a message for anyone who didn't answer. She left out the part of our first date, knowing they would flip out before they had a chance to meet me or hear the entire story. Their reactions were slightly enthusiastic, yet still skeptical since none of them had the pleasure to meet me at this point. I was still very new to the picture and they had heard little, if anything, about me up until this point.

Larissa didn't have any luck when she attempted to reach Bobby, one of her older brothers. He lived in Atlanta at the time and was on his way to Pennsylvania. He wasn't on his way specifically to see me, but coincidence has it he was going to be doing some work on a nearby church he was affiliated with. He had seen Larissa's tweet about seeing Owen Wilson which made him raise an eyebrow since he knew it was highly unlikely she would have seen Owen Wilson in Lancaster for any reason. He did some investigating on Facebook and found my profile. Larissa had mentioned to him about me prior to our date, so he had a pretty solid idea on where he should start digging.

Bobby uncovered the status I had posted about fly-ing into the sunset, followed by several pictures I posted of Me and Larissa at several locations that were obviously not Lancaster. When he realized I had taken his little sister to California, he couldn't help but be concerned, and that's put-ting it lightly. He was nearly livid. He had to be sure Larissa was making good decisions now that she was independently living in Lancaster, away from all of her family. If he didn't already have plans to come to Lancaster, he would have been making immediate plans to do so.

The next couple days I was flooded with work, but I wanted to be sure I had the chance to meet Bobby before he returned to Atlanta. If I didn't make an effort to, he would have tracked me down and found me before he left. I figured it always looks better to show initiative than to wait for him to find me. Especially with the way I had begun my relationship with his sister. At this point, I didn't think her family knew anything about our first date, but with Bobby being in the area, the likelihood seemed much higher that he may be aware of what was going on. I wasn't too concerned, considering I had nothing but good intentions with Larissa.

While I was out doing fieldwork on the tractor I received a text from Drew. "Want to come to Prince Street Cafe to meet Bobby?" it read.

"Yeah, I'd love to! I'll be there when I finish up work." I texted him. I was sure this was going to be interesting. This would be the first family member of Larissa's that I would have the chance to meet and I really wanted to leave a good impression. I was looking forward to getting to know her family and this would be my first opportunity. When I finished work, I cleaned up and headed to Lancaster City.

When I arrived at Prince Street Cafe I was full of every bit of confidence. Of course, taking a girl on a surprise date to California can graciously boost one's ego. I was not only confident from the accomplishment of our first date, but because I knew I had absolutely nothing to worry about. My intentions were pure. I didn't take Larissa to California for any improper reasons, I took her there for the adventure. Since I didn't have any bad intentions, there was no reason for me to be afraid.

I confidently walked through the door and saw Larissa, Drew, Drew's cousin Daniel, and Bobby. Bobby had blazing red hair, stood at the same height, yet was clearly far more muscular. He was working as a Deputy at a county jail in Georgia at the time, and he was used to keeping the inmates of Atlanta in line, breaking up fights when he needed to. Bobby sat at the table with his knuckles intertwined and elbows on the table doing his best to intimidate me from the beginning of our interaction. His glare was unable to pierce my armor of confidence as I walked up to the table and extended my hand, expecting to give him a firm handshake. He kept his hands where they were, leaving me to stand awkwardly with my hand out, only to receive no return of a friendly gesture.

"Sit down." He said with a commanding tone. Bobby was being direct and firm with me but I wasn't phased. I sat down next to Larissa and smiled reassuringly toward her. Drew was sitting to the left of us with a bit of a grin on his face. After his failed attempts to prevent our first date from happening, I could tell he was looking forward to seeing everything blow up in my face. This meeting was pure entertainment for him.

I remained confident while doing my best to not come across as cocky. "It's a pleasure to meet you." I said. "Larissa speaks very highly of you."

"I know she does." He replied abruptly without even the slightest smirk on his face. "So tell me a little about yourself."

This was a good place for me to start, since I had such a great " life resume". This would be great way to build credibility.

"Well, I was born and raised in a Christian home on a dairy farm. I've been a Christian since I was in middle school.

I enjoy extreme sports like rock climbing, snowboarding, and surfing. I lived in Los Angeles for a year not long after I graduated high school. When I moved back to the farm I started volunteering as a leader for a ministry called Young Life. I spend a lot of my spare time with teens who go to the local high school. I try to be a positive influence and share Christ with them." I could tell he was reading deep into my every word, looking for any hint of an effort to be deceptive.

"Why do you like my sister?" He asked while continuing to be as intimidating as possible. Now I knew he was really beating around the bush. I knew why he was here, and what he really wanted to know. I was sure he wanted to see if I was too scared to bring up my first date with Larissa without him having to pry for an explanation. I knew any effort to beat around the bush on my part to avoid talking about it would make him feel like I was trying to hide something, and I was certain that wouldn't rub him well. I was beginning to feel that if I was showing any hint of a slightly wrong intention he was ready to punch me across the face hard enough to throw me to the floor of the cafe.

"I think she is really awesome." I responded. "She has so much energy and a sense for adventure. I admire how she loves the Lord, and strives to glorify God in the way she lives her life. Soon after I had met her, while we were texting, she told me she was the most awesomest thing God put on the planet. And you know, for some reason, I was feeling convinced that what she was saying just might be true."

I paused briefly as I prepared to transition into an explanation of why I took Larissa across the country for our first date. "Last weekend I took Larissa to Los Angeles for our first date. The reason I took her there was simply because nothing else made sense. It didn't make any sense to take 'the most awesomest girl that God put on the planet' out on a date as if she was just an ordinary girl. I wouldn't have been comfortable taking her anywhere that I hadn't been before, or where I didn't know anybody. To me, LA is simply a second home. I lived there for over a year, and I have several friends there. I made sure we had separate sleeping arrangements and told her if she wasn't comfortable staying with my friends, I'd get her a hotel room for herself."

My answer felt long winded, but I stacked it with every relevant piece of information that would put the cards in my favor. Every bit of what I had to say was true. I spoke with full confidence in the decision that I had made.

I continued on, doing my best to hold onto this positive momentum. "You have a really awesome sister, I'm sure you realize that. I'm especially thankful to see that she has a brother like you, who cares enough about her to sit down with me to make sure I'm a good guy, and that she's making wise decisions on who she is dating. I can't thank you enough for being here and watching out for her, because not every girl has that. I really would like the opportunity to get to know you and the rest of your family, because that is huge to me. I want to make sure your entire family is comfortable with me, now that we are dating."

Bobby pursed his lips and nodded slightly. In a weird way my logic for taking her to Los Angeles was beginning to make sense, which was the last thing he ever expected. "Well, that was really a crazy thing to do. You do seem to be a good, upright guy, even though really had me very feeling very skeptical and nervous. I'll be staying in contact to make sure you're taking good care of my sister."

I could tell Bobby was no longer putting up a front and beginning to become more relaxed. The hard part was over. Now he was no longer playing "hardball" and genuinely seemed more interested in getting to know me on a more personal level. "So you trained to be a stunt driver, huh?" He asked.

"Yeah, I did. I loved living in California, but when I realized I wasn't pursuing after it like I really wanted to truly succeed, I decided it was time to come home. I still question my decision sometimes." I said jokingly.

"How many speeding tickets have you gotten?" Bobby had a pretty big grin on his face as he asked. It seemed like he was convinced he would have more than I did. I wasn't so convinced.

"I've had 6 moving violations in 5 different states." I said with a grin. "How about you?" In my mind I was already convinced I would be the winner of this small contest.

"I've had 7 speeding tickets. All of them were on the same cross country trip." He said. He then went on telling the story of how he had gotten them, which included well thought out sound effects, facial expressions, and bits of laughter. I could see where Larissa had picked up on such an ability to tell a lively story.

"How old are you?" asked Bobby

"I'm 24" I replied.

"When do you Turn 25?"

"In September"

"Okay, good" Bobby jeered, as the four months ahead of me proved to be another form of dominance.

Our meeting had officially transformed from an interrogation into a conversation. Now it was a contest of "who is better than who" as we took turns swapping manly stories trying to outgun the other. We laughed as we went back and forth.

Bobby seemed like an awesome guy. Our conversation was full of laughter as it sparked the several stories we had to offer. What I found most interesting was meeting this guy who Larissa grew up with and seeing what characteristics had rubbed off on her. I could see so much similarity in their sense of humor, their laughter, and most of all their confidence. The origins of many of her characteristics were beginning to become evident.

After plenty of talking, swapping stories and lots of laughter, we made our way out of the Cafe. Before we parted, Bobby concluded "You do seem like a really good guy, Tom. I'm definitely glad we were able to get together and talk things through. I'm going to put in a good word to my dad that you're an upright guy, so you can get on his good side. He trusts my judgement and my opinions will go a long way. See if you can give him a call, and try to make a trip up there as soon as you get the chance, so he can get to know you."

"I certainly will, man." I responded to him with sincerity. "Thanks for meeting me here tonight. It was a pleasure to meet you and I really would appreciate you putting a good word in for me. It means a lot. I'll stay in touch with you as well. Hopefully we can get together again sometime soon."

As I climbed into my Subaru and began my drive home, I thought about how great it was to meet Bobby. He seemed like the kind of guy I could really become great friends with. He had the same sense of adventure, we shared many hobbies, and he seemed like he was up for anything. I thought about how I wanted to try and get together with him more often and maybe include him on some kind of adventure. I knew snowboarding was something he was already into. I knew rock climbing would be something he might enjoy. Not to mention he talked about how he had never been to California and really wanted to go there. I was really excited for not only getting to know Larissa more, but for the opportunity to get to know the rest of her family.

●　　●　　●

Something people all too often don't realize is that when you're dating somebody, you're also dating their family, and when you marry someone, you also marry their family. Good relations with a family are especially important, and will benefit you immensely in the long run. Families want to see their son or daughter with someone they can know and trust. If you break that trust, it can make things more difficult for your relationship, and if your relationship survives, fixing these severed ties can take years.

Having great relations with a special individual's family starts with who you are as a person. Are you trustworthy? What are your intentions? Are you being genuine? Is there something you're trying to hide?

Think hard on these questions, because if you can't be trusted, or if you have selfish intentions and you feel the need to hide the person you really are, you need to focus on getting yourself where you need to be before ever getting into a relationship. You should never allow yourself to be defined by a relationship, but the relationship is defined by the people who are in it, and where their values stand.

Never allow yourself to depend on another person to change you into who you need to be. It should be up to you to make sure you have a solid grip of who you are before dating someone. It can take time, and for some, longer than others.

In the first chapter I talked about how I had spent my life trying to find out who I would marry. I was looking to find the relationship that would define me. It wasn't until I learned to trust God with my future that I was able to live my life defined by his will, that Larissa was brought into my life, and the timing couldn't have been better. When you allow yourself to be molded by God, that is when you find yourself living the incredible life He has planned for you.

After I let go of my selfish desires, and fully trusted God with his plans for my life, I stumbled into a relationship with Larissa that was clearly defined by God, and each of us as individuals in the way He had been working in our hearts and minds. Taking Larissa to California for our first date didn't turn me into an adventurous person. It didn't turn her into an adventurous person either. Our relationship is truly a reflection of who God made us to be. We were two adventurous individuals who God brought together and gave us a relationship that perfectly reflects the people He made us to be.

If I hadn't been confident in who I am as a person, with strong morals, and good intentions, I have no doubt Bobby would have seen right through it. He would have been sure to warn the rest of the family, including her father, that I was bad news. I had already put myself on a thin wire by taking her to California for our first date. It's only by God's grace that He brought all the right elements together to make that work in a way that I was able to balance that fine line and accomplish such a feat so I could gain trust and respect from her family afterwards.

● ● ●

CHAPTER 6
I Love You

"I love you" is a phrase I don't take lightly. The last time I had said those powerful words to a girl was in high school when I was making a last ditch effort to save a dying relationship. Not only did I fail to save the relationship, but it served as the final nail on the coffin. After realizing it wasn't a phrase to be taken lightly, I made a commitment to be sure I was in love with the person I said it to.

Larissa and I were a few weeks into this blissful dating relationship. I could tell it was different than any romantic relationship I had ever been in. All two of them. As I had been getting to know Larissa, and trusting God with whatever role she might have in my life, I was doing my best not to jump ahead of myself with any assumption that Larissa would be my future wife. Even though the first date had come together flawlessly, and our relationship was in full blossom, I wanted to make sure I could trust God if He did, in fact, intend for me to be single for the rest of my life. Not to mention, in my past relationships I had scared off my girlfriends by taking the relationship way too seriously and talking as though we would get married someday. I wanted to make sure I was thinking clearly and taking things one step at a time. More than anything else, I hate being wrong.

As much as I was doing my best to proceed in our relationship with caution, things certainly seemed to be different than what I had in the past. Not to mention, she was more awesome than any girl I had ever known, and I couldn't imagine the possibility of a more awesome guy for her to be with either. The level of affection we were experiencing was incredibly mutual, and that was a warm, new feeling.

Larissa and I managed to find time to spend together every day since we had started dating. She would hang out with me at work, and we continued our tradition of watching movies and talking for hours afterwards. I never before had so much fun getting to know someone.

One night, after hours of talking and spending the day together, a crazy, unexpected thing happened. It was getting late in the evening on a Saturday night and I had to milk early in the morning. I walked her out onto the porch and hugged her for a few moments. This was the part of our day we were both learning to resent. The part where we had to say goodbye.

"Goodnight." I said as I looked into her beautiful brown eyes. "I hope you rest well tonight. I'll see you in the morning before church."

She looked at me and smiled. "Okay I'll see you then. Goodnight. I love you." She blurted out before she had the chance stop the words from coming out of her mouth.

I looked at her. Confused. I wasn't 100% sure of what she just said. I thought she might have said "I love you" but it didn't fully register in my mind. I raised my eyebrows in question. "Wait. Did you just say-"

"No" she cut me off. Her eyes were as wide as a deer in the headlights of an oncoming car. She was in full panic mode, doing her best to apply some damage control. "I didn't say anything. Goodnight!"

Larissa turned around and bolted out the door. I thought about running after her to get this figured out. What she said wasn't fully registering because it had caught me by such surprise. *Did she just say 'I love you'?* I thought to myself trying to comprehend what had just happened. I stood there, still confused. Meanwhile I could see her Mitsubishi Eclipse come flying down the stone driveway from where she had parked. The uneven section where we normally drive slow was taken with no caution whatsoever. The car mercilessly bottomed out on the driveway as though her life was in jeopardy. I thought about jumping on my motorcycle and chasing her down, but I was still trying to comprehend what had actually happened. On one hand it seemed like she was running away, but on the other hand, that kind of driving wasn't necessarily anything out of the ordinary for her. If I had known for sure that she had said "I love you" I certainly would have jumped on my motorcycle, and chased her down so I could say it back.

I walked up to my room while still trying to wrap my mind around what had just happened. What she had said was only beginning to register in my mind, as I was becoming more confident in what she had said.

Not even a minute later, I received a text from Larissa. "That wasn't what it sounded like." That was all the affirmation I needed. She definitely said "I love you." She said it before I did. I was out of the "danger zone" of having to take the dangerous leap of faith by saying it first. Now I didn't have to worry about putting myself out there by saying those three words, risking the potential responses like "Thank you" or "I know" or "Me too."

My phone buzzed once more and the next text read "I'm sorry." More affirmation. Now how was I supposed to fix this to allow her to fall asleep? Texting her back with "I love you" certainly didn't seem appropriate. I certainly didn't want to say it over text for the first time either. Whatever I did, I had to be careful. Last thing I wanted was for her to pack her things overnight and move back to New York in a state of panic.

"Ok. Goodnight :) " I responded. I wasn't sure how to say "I love you" without saying "I love you." It was difficult coming up with a good response without making things weird. I figured I could talk to her about it in the morning before church.

I couldn't help but smile and find the humor in what had just happened. This was new to me. I had never been told "I love you" by a girl I liked. As I have already mentioned, It wasn't a term I threw around frivolously, either. I learned that lesson in high school. When I said it to my girlfriend when I was in high school, it not only served as the final nail on the coffin of our relationship, but it was another prime example of my focus on finding a wife. I had told her I loved her after she was starting to get freaked out because of my desire for a serious relationship. Yikes!

Fortunately I can confidently say that after I learned that lesson, I refrained from using those meaningful words anytime afterwards. Even as Larissa and I were on our crazy

California adventure at the beginning of our relationship I was careful not to say it. Even throughout the first couple weeks, as the words continually came to my mind, I carefully processed my vocabulary every time we said "goodbye".

So here I was. Larissa had accidentally told me she loved me and I didn't even have the chance to say it back. Now I had time to think about it. Did I love her? I certainly felt like I did. I knew I had to keep myself from saying it every time we said goodbye. By this point I was becoming very convinced that this was the girl I would be spending the rest of my life with. I couldn't imagine any better girl out there for me. Did I love her? Of course I did. I certainly didn't want her to feel as though she put herself out there and was rejected. I hated the thought of her feeling that way. I loved her enough to know I didn't want her to feel alone in this. I had to tell her.

The next morning Larissa came over early enough to ride to church with me. I could tell something seemed a little off. She acted nervous, and a little awkward.

"I want to talk about what happened last night." I told her.

"Huh? Nothing. I mean, nothing happened" she said as she desperately tried to avoid the subject and turned her head trying to look at anything but me. Her wide eyes darted from one end of the room to another.

I reached for her arm and brought her closer to me. "Look." I said as she looked around the room trying her best to avoid eye contact. "Did you tell me you loved me last night when you left?" Now she was really getting fidgety. It was really seeming like she wanted out of this conversation more than anything else in her life at the time. "Seriously, did you tell me you loved me?" I inquired again as she continued to look around in desperation in hopes to find a way out. I stepped closer as I held onto both of her hands to prevent her from getting away from me as she lightly squirmed in an attempt to break loose from this terrifying conversation. "I just want you to know that you're not alone." I started reassuring her best I could. "I love you too."

Her struggle stopped. She held perfectly still and looked up at me. "Are you sure?" she asked me as I could sense the fear resonating in her voice.

"Yes I'm sure!" I laughed. "You're awesome, and I really love you. You can relax, because you're not alone in this, I love you!"

Her look of terror faded and it turned into a smile that reached her eyes. I hugged her and held her tight. This was awesome. For the first time in my life I was in love, and I couldn't imagine anybody better to be in love with.

• • •

Now here is a challenging question: When is the right time to tell someone you love them? Is there a right answer? I think the real question is: "How many people do you want to tell you love them before you eventually say it to your spouse?" By the time you find your spouse, do you want that life changing phrase to be overused and meaningless? If you say it to every person you're in a relationship with, how do you differentiate the fact that you sincerely mean it by the time you find the person you want to spend the rest of your life with?

How much meaning do you want it to have when you finally tell someone you love them? I think that's the question everybody needs to ask themselves before they jump the gun and tell that to someone for the first time. If the phrase is used in every relationship you've ever been in, it's difficult to retain the value of the phrase. Recognizing the value of those words is important. They are more than words.

So when is the right time to tell someone you love them? It's different for everybody. Larissa said it a few weeks into our relationship. To most people that's very fast. She said it because it was what she was always thinking, and prevented herself from saying it until she couldn't help it anymore and it slipped out. If you're trying to decide if you should say it, it's likely not the right time, or the right person. If you are able to save those words for your future spouse, it gives the phrase much more sincerity and meaning.

● ● ●

Larissa and I loved each other and that seemed to be clearly established. We had successfully powered through to the next level of our relationship with every bit of fast paced momentum this love scene was carrying. Not even a week later, we were already discussing a future together. It was becoming clear to us this relationship was a permanent thing.

Now my mind was churning. I had a new problem on my hands. How was I going to propose to the love of my life? I had already taken her to California for our first date. Now I had to come up with something brilliant to outdo that. She certainly deserved the best. I thought of a good place and it made sense. When I lived in Los Angeles there was a hike beginning at Brand Library Park in Glendale that provided beautiful views of city lights three quarters of the way around where you stood at the scenic viewpoint. Of course, getting to that viewpoint was a long, treacherous hike, but the view was beyond worth it.

When I lived in California, this was one of my favorite hikes, and I had gone up a handful of times. I had even taken Jordan to see it when he came out to help me move home, and when I did my road trip with Cameron and the other graduates, I had taken them on the hike as well. It was certainly one of the most breathtaking views I had ever seen, and I never grew tired of it.

On our first date I kept the idea of her potentially being my wife someday out of my mind, but just in case she would be, I didn't take her on this hike. I wanted to at least reserve this as an option to propose to her, so it would be somewhere she hadn't already been to. In the back of my mind I had always thought it would be an excellent place to propose to the woman God had chosen for me, but when I was living in Pennsylvania it no longer seemed to be a feasible option.

Now that I had met Larissa and our relationship was a whirlwind of adventure, taking her there so I could propose seemed to be the ideal location. Since Larissa and I had gone to Los Angeles for our first date, the city now had a lot of meaning to us. Taking her to this hike would certainly be the best possible location for me to propose.

I knew this would be perfect, but now I had another obstacle to overcome. How was I going to get her out to California to propose to her? If I tried to pull another "Surprise, we're going to Los Angeles!" she would already know. There wouldn't be any other reason for me to take her out there again. Hands down, I needed to find some other way to get her out to Los Angeles, and somehow propose to her without her expecting it.

One evening Larissa and I were spending time together and we were discussing our future. We knew we wanted to get married, so we pondered if it was something we should take our time getting to that point, or just get it done and over with. We decided to start making a list of pros and cons on whether or not we should elope. After all, it seemed as though all of our friends were expecting we would. They knew we were made for eachother, and we were crazy enough to do something so outrageous. Our friends were often making jokes about the fact that we were totally going to elope and how they wouldn't be surprised.

Certain aspects of eloping did make a lot of sense. On the pros side, she would no longer have to drive home every night, and we would probably be able to snag the house I wanted on the farm. We were convinced we would probably save a whole heap of money by not having a legitimate wedding ceremony. The idea of spending the rest of our lives together was incredibly exciting, too. If we could speed up the process to make that happen, it would be much easier to enjoy numerous adventures together.

We listed out the cons. They were certainly hard to think of. After all, what list of conveniences are there to putting off getting married to your soul mate? The reasons we came up with were mostly for the sake of other people. Not eloping and taking our time would likely keep both of our families rather happy. We would also be giving up the opportunity to get lots of free stuff. From what we heard, throwing a wedding paid out quite well. Also, if we had a wedding, we would be able to see several of our friends and relatives. Having them all there to share such a great moment would be wonderful. We also felt there were several things God wanted to teach us through our relationship, and if we were going to be getting married, why shouldn't we be open to enjoying this time period God has set out for us and spiritually prepare for marriage best we could?

The biggest voice of reason speaking into my subconscious was the fact that I had two older sisters that had gotten married and at the time, my parents were not thrilled with the men they were marrying. The largest disadvantage to eloping would be that I couldn't give my parents a wedding they could look forward to, which they had yet to experience.

Together we decided against eloping, but something clicked in my mind. A stroke of genus! I figured out a way to get Larissa out to Los Angeles again without her expecting me to propose to her! "I have a great idea!" I exclaimed to Larissa. "Why don't we fake elope?! It'd be hilarious! After all, it's what everybody really wants to see! Everyone keeps bringing it up, since we went to California for our first date. Why don't we just give them what they really want to see!"

Her eyes lit up "That sounds like an awesome idea! It's so crazy. I don't think that's ever been done before. We should totally do that!"

We both laughed at this crazy idea. We joked about how people would react. We were now convinced this was the greatest idea we had ever come up with. Little did she know, the idea of fake eloping was just a distractraction. It was a minor part of my greater plan. And her agreeing to fake elope with me was a giant leap forward. This would give me the opportunity to take her to LA without expecting me to propose to her.

We started plotting. The plan was to fly to Las Vegas and go to a touristy spot. Larissa would be wearing a white dress. Not a wedding dress, but a nice dressy white dress. I would be wearing a suit, vest and tie. Just a little bit classier than a plain suit, but not quite as classy as a tuxedo. We would find an Elvis impersonator on the street and get him to hold a bible to make it look as though he was officiating a wedding.

The Idea was not to say that we had gotten married. We were going to post photos to social media and allow people to assume what they wanted. There's no dishonesty in that, right?

So we talked about what else we would do while we were out west. Of course if we were in Las Vegas we couldn't NOT go to Los Angeles. It was only 4 hours away. We figured we could swing down there and visit my friends again. She agreed to the idea and I knew I was locked in. This was my chance to get her back to Los Angeles for a proposal.

I figured after the fake elopement and the engagement we would need a place to catch our breath and contact our friends and family about the news while the dust settled. My cousin Glenda lived in Sacramento and she was always happy to have me visit. I knew she would love to have us there for that time. Sacramento wasn't too close to LA or Vegas, but I figured we would just make an epic road trip out of it.

Larissa agreed to the idea of making it a big trip and seeing Glenda while we were in California. Now, if we were driving from LA to Sacramento, we may as well drive along the Pacific Coastal Highway to see some of the most beautiful views the west coast has to offer. So there we were. We had assembled a plan. We would fly to Las Vegas, fake elope, drive to LA, then drive up the coast, go through San Francisco and visit Glenda in Sacramento. After a couple days, we would drive back to Vegas and fly home. Just like that, our crazy idea had transformed into plans of a solid adventure.

It was late April and we needed to decide what would be the best time to pull this off. We decided we would do this on the weekend of my birthday, September 21. This way corn would certainly be harvested and we would have a window of time to go do this before my family left for Idaho to go hunting in the beginning of October. We had a decent amount of time until then, and sure, things might not work out and this whole idea could blow up in my face, but I shrugged it off. I had already taken bigger risks. The first date hadn't blown up in my face like it easily could have, and things worked out perfectly. So what's the harm in putting this plan together? Larissa was already agreeing to it, so I trusted my gut feeling and pushed forward with putting this plan into motion.

Right away we called Glenda to see if it would suit her for us to stay at her place for a few days. We explained the whole idea to her and she laughed. She was used to my crazy antics and was always very supportive. She is always an incredible host, making sure I always felt welcomed. Any time I was in California I would do my best to visit her and the kids. She told us the dates we chose worked well for her and she would love to have us there to visit, just as I knew she would.

Larissa and I began to look up some airline tickets on the computer. Flying to Vegas wouldn't be very expensive. We found some sweet deals with the right flight times and I was ready to pull out my credit card and lock them in.

"Wait." Larissa stopped me. "Something doesn't feel quite right. Let's hold off on buying the tickets for now."

"Alright" I told her. I didn't quite understand, considering how on board she was with the whole idea, but I didn't want to push her into something she wasn't comfortable with. I figured we could just sleep on it and we would get the tickets later.

It was getting late and Larissa needed a ride home, since her car getting worked on. As I drove her to Lancaster and we talked more about our crazy idea. The thought of fake-eloping was very appealing to us, as we joked about how absurd of an idea it really was.

I dropped her off and wished her a goodnight. While driving home I kept pondering my genius idea. As I was thinking about how this would play out I suddenly began to feel a strong conviction. According to our itinerary we would be driving almost 1500 miles. As fun as it would be, we would certainly be spending a lot of time by ourselves in a car in unfamiliar places. When we flew to Los Angeles for our first date, we were spending most of our time with friends in a place very familiar to me. A city I call my second home. The fake elopement idea involved several hours of driving between locations and spending time in places neither of us had been before.

On our first date, we were so fresh into our relationship, sexual temptation was almost non-existent. Besides the fact that our relationship was new, we were spending so much time around my friends, we weren't even giving temptation a chance. With the accelerated pace our relationship was currently taking, I knew we would be facing an exponential amount of temptation by the time we would be doing our fake-eloping trip. Couple that with several hours alone in a car in unfamiliar places, and we would be subjecting ourselves to more temptation than ever before. I was suddenly growing very uncomfortable with the concept of us going on such an adventure by ourselves. As the idea of doing such an adventure with only Larissa was clearly not a good idea, I realized we wouldn't face nearly as much, if any temptation if we had accountability with us. I knew having accountability was not only very important, but it would send a clear message to all of our friends, family, and my Young Life students that we were striving for purity in our relationship.

The next day I brought my concerns up to Larissa. Coincidentally, she was feeling the same exact conviction that night as well. Clearly God was telling us what He wanted. The fake elopement was still an excellent concept, but only if we had someone along to keep us accountable. When we understood we had simultaneously experienced the same conviction, we understood what we needed to do, and we suddenly felt at peace about going about our plan.

Larissa and I began to discuss who we might talk to about coming with us on this trip. The first person to come to my mind was Cameron Anderson, Drew's younger brother. Cameron was no stranger to my crazy antics and adventurous mindset. I spent a lot of time mentoring him while he was in high school. After he graduated, I took him and two other guys on a road trip to California. Our trip involved a lot of rock climbing, hiking, road biking, and surfing. The four of us piled all of our gear into my Subaru Legacy, barely fitting our essentials into the trunk. We mounted three bikes and two surfboards on the thule roof rack, which my car proudly wore like a crown. I recalled how much fun it was to be on a road trip with Cameron. He made the best of every moment, maintaining an impressively positive attitude in every situation, even though spending three weeks primarily in a sedan with three other guys can make it easy to knock heads and egos from time to time. Cameron loved adventure, crazy ideas, making jokes, and maintained a seemingly endless source of enthusiasm. I knew he would be the perfect person to talk to about joining us for the fake eloping trip.

Larissa and I also talked about inviting Bobby to join us. I had only met him once, but he seemed as though he would be down to join us for this kind of adventure. Although, since he was Larissa's brother, it would likely be less weird if we waited a couple months into our relationship to present the idea to him rather than right away, which it had only been a couple weeks.

Since Cameron was more accustomed to my crazy antics, we decided to talk to him immediately, so we at least knew we had the accountability we needed to move forward with this mission.

I invited Cameron to hang out with me and Larissa for the evening. We went up to my room. Larissa and I sat down across from him. "Cameron" I began. "There's something we want to talk to you about. But we first need to know that we can trust you."

"Okay" He said with a chuckle as a large grin spread across his face. I hadn't even started to hint at our plan, but he had learned how to tell if I was about to tell him about a crazy idea.

"When I told you I would be taking Larissa to California for our first date, Drew overheard as you were telling your mom about what I was doing. He was really nervous about it and came pretty close on a few occasions to ruining the surprise for Larissa. He made an effort to tell her but fortunately Larissa wouldn't allow him to. We want to include you in a plan we have put together, but this is something you're not allowed to tell anybody about. Absolutely no one. Do you understand?"

"Yes I understand." Cameron said as he maintained the grin on his face. I was sure he could sense another one of my crazy ideas coming.

"Okay. As long as we're in agreement here and understand this is a big secret, and absolutely nobody is to know about this. Not even your parents." I affirmed with him.

Larissa and I looked at eachother as I continued. She was as excited to tell him as I was. "In September we are planning to fly to Las Vegas." I started. "Now why do you think we would be flying to Las Vegas?"

The grin on his face was nearly large enough to make his head explode. "Um. Does it have to do with this box right here?" He glanced towards the small black felt box I had conveniently placed right next to where he would be sitting, just to mess with him. It was only a box for my cuff links, but it almost looked like it was made for a wedding ring.

"No, but close." I said with a grin. "That's exactly what we want everybody to think. Everybody thinks that me and Larissa are going to elope. We decided we're going to give everybody what they want to see and make them think we eloped. We're going to fake-elope" I stated, clearly outlining the plan to him.

Cameron burst out in laughter, just as I knew he would. Of course the idea was absurd, but he loved the idea.

"Our plan is to fly to Las Vegas" I continued explaining the itinerary, "Larissa and I are going to pretend to elope and put photos of it up on social media. After the fake elopement we're going to drive to LA and spend a day there, then drive up the pacific coastal highway to Sacramento to visit Glenda. After a few days with Glenda, we'll drive back to Las Vegas and fly home."

Cameron was still laughing. He calmed down after a moment as he finally managed to ask "So why are you telling me about this? Is there something you need me to do to help?" He inquired as he tried to contain his laughter.

I then explained to him "Larissa and I feel strongly that we should have some accountability with us for the trip. What we're wondering is.." Larissa and I glanced at each other as we both got down on one knee in front of him as we proposed this idea to him. I grabbed the small black felt box containing my cuff links. I opened it and held it out to him as if it was an actual ring. "...Will you fake elope with us?"

"Yes! Yes, I'll fake elope with you!" He exclaimed with excitement pretending as though he was a young girl that had just been offered a shiny diamond ring. Cameron was laughing so hard at this point he could barely contain it.

Solid. The plan was set in motion. Larissa and I had the accountability we needed to join us for the trip, and the gut feeling which was hindering us earlier was completely removed. We logged onto my computer and searched for airline tickets. We found some great deals for our flights in September and immediately purchased the tickets. We would be flying out on a Saturday night and flying back that next Wednesday. We all had our agreement of secrecy and we were really pumped about our plan. We were not going to tell anyone about this. Not even our best friends. And we would have to keep this big secret to ourselves for the extent of our entire dating relationship.

After our flights were locked in, I was feeling incredibly accomplished. Not only had I taken Larissa across the country for our first date, but I had an incredible plan to propose to her that was falling perfectly into place.

● ● ●

Accountability is highly underrated. If I could make any changes to our dating relationship I would have made an effort to focus more of our time to be spent with groups of friends, or even by spending more time out in public. Sexual temptation can be very strong when you're in a dating relationship. It's much stronger when you allow yourself to be alone more often than you need to be.

It's still easy to get to know a person when you're with them in a group. Sometimes it's even more enjoyable since it provides a casual setting and removes the sexual temptation entirely, giving you the chance to get to know them and see how they interact with other people. Sexual temptation is only as strong as you allow it to be. While Larissa and I were able to resist the temptation to have sex before we were married, our relationship would have been more enjoyable if we spent more time with other people. I'm thankful we made the decision to have accountability with us when we did our fake-elopement trip. Going as a group allowed us to have lots of fun, and we didn't face any temptation on the trip whatsoever, which made it even better.

● ● ●

CHAPTER 7
The Blessing

Larissa and I had gone to LA for our first date, we were in love, and I had a plan in motion to propose to her. At this point, I was certainly overdue to meet her parents, though finding time to go visit them proved to be difficult- at least this time of the year. It was Spring, which tends to be the busiest season of the year when you're a farmer. So instead, Larissa and I called her dad within a week after meeting with Bobby, so he could start getting to know me. Bobby had already spoken to him and given him an "all clear," informing him that I was an upright guy.

As we spoke on the phone, Larissa's dad, or Mr. Sutton as I know him, sounded like a man getting along in years, but spoke in a joyful way. He asked about my personal background, the farm my family owned, and the work I had going on at the time. He was blown away by how large my family's farm was. Everything was exciting to him! Our conversation was filled with his reactions of "Oh, Wow!" and "Good, good" as well as the occasional laughter. He told me about how highly Bobby had spoken of me and asked when I would have a chance to visit. Being a farmer himself, he was very understanding of the fact that it was a busy time of the year for us on the farm, and encouraged me to visit when I had the chance. I told him we would certainly be visiting as soon as we could catch a break from the hard work on our farm. The farm where he lived was in the Catskills, in upstate New York. They milked nearly thirty cows using a very outdated milking system.

My conversation with Mr. Sutton was very successful. Nothing was brought up about our first date, and I was sure if he had any knowledge about it he would have asked. To him, I was a huge blessing. I was a farmer from Lancaster, Pennsylvania, which to him was upheld as if it was the 'holy land' of farming, and I managed to gain the attention of Larissa. Larissa had always promised herself she would never marry a farmer, and she wasn't afraid to make it known. She couldn't wait to leave her family's farm in New York, only to end up dating a guy who had a farm at least ten times as large.

Two months after Larissa and I started dating, we eventually found a weekend that worked for us to visit her family so I had the opportunity to meet them. I knew I wanted this to go flawlessly, since Larissa and I were very serious about our relationship. When I spoke to Mr. Sutton over the phone, the joyful tone in his voice was full of laughter, but Larissa had told me stories about how he could often be a very stern man when he needed to be. The household he ran was very strict in a way that reflected old-order mennonites or even Amish. In fact, there was one point he had actually considered moving to Lancaster County and joining the Amish church.

I've always been great at meeting parents- anybody's parents. Just a few minutes of conversation and they knew I was trustworthy. This time was different. I wasn't just a guy she was dating, I was the guy who whisked their daughter away to California for our first date. I didn't want to leave anything to chance. I was determined not to allow our first date to screw up my ability to gain acceptance and become one of the worst mistakes of my life.

Since I'm so full of great ideas, I convinced my parents to come with us to visit her family. I knew my parents would not only vouch for me, but I was certain if Mr. Sutton had the opportunity to meet those who raised me, he would be more comfortable about my relationship with Larissa. Additionally, my dad would be able talk with him non-stop about farming and everything that came with it, so they would be sure to find plenty of common ground. Meanwhile, my mom would get to know Mrs. Sutton, another farmer's wife she could relate to.

I had already set a timeline for when I wanted to propose, so I needed to gain the trust and approval of her family as quickly and efficiently as possible. Otherwise my plans would completely crumble.

Larissa's sister, Kate was set to get married early in September. My plan was to ask for Mr. Sutton's blessing when we came for the wedding, which at this point was a brief four months away. My parents would not only be reinforcements, but they would help me gain the trust of Larissa's family at an accelerated pace.

When the weekend came to make our visit, Larissa and I climbed into my parents van and were able to take it easy as my dad drove. The drive was taking unusually long, according to Larissa. Apparently what was supposed to be a five hour drive had turned into eight hours, so my dad could avoid paying $2 in tolls (I'm sure it was worth the detour). After what felt like ages we arrived at her family's home.

So here we were pulling up to her parent's house in the middle of podunk Upstate New York. Looking around the farm it felt like we stepped back in time. Old equipment lay scattered around, corroding, just as I was used to seeing on my family's farm. The milking barn's classic red paint was weathered and the tin roof had sections of rust showing it's age.

As we pulled into the stone driveway, her family started coming out from just about everywhere to greet us. Mary was the first to come out to us. Her dirty blonde hair was long and braided down her back, she wore a long skirt and was dressed conservatively. Katie came out of the barn. Her hair was medium length and dark brown. She was also wearing long skirt and dressed conservatively as well. I was beginning to sense a pattern here. Many of Larissa's old photos I had previously seen on Facebook, when I was curiously looking deep into her profile, were beginning to make sense.

Larissa's parents stepped out of the house with large smiles on their faces. It was clear they were happy to see us. Her mom had long white/silver hair to her waist and a friendly smile on her face. Larissa's dad had a rounded face, with ruddy complexion, you could see where time was carving out its signature around his face. The wrinkles on his face were most prominent in the areas critical for a good smile. Beneath his smiling eyes and wide grin, he grew a lengthy reddish-grey beard. He was dressed in his work clothes, that you could tell had seen long hours of work over the years. When I shook his hand, the rough surface reflected the life of a hard-working man.

Larissa's other sister, Tesla drove up to the house only a few minutes later, dressed casually in jeans and a t-shirt. She introduced herself cautiously as I gave her a warm handshake.

After a few moments of greeting one another, Mrs. Sutton brought the meal out she had prepared. It was a nice day, so we sat down at the picnic table outside. Before eating, we sang a couple of classic hymns. Not a meal tradition I was used to, but I grew up singing hymns in a traditional church service, so I was fortunately able to sing right along without any hesitation.

Once we finished singing, we all joined hands as Mr. Sutton began to bless the meal. It took all my effort to keep my eyes closed and not exchange glances with Larissa. I could feel her trying to sneak in some eye contact. The way she teasingly squeezed my hand certainly didn't make things any easier. Last thing I wanted to do was laugh during prayer. As the prayer went on for a few minutes, all I could think about was a conversation Larissa and I recently had as she was preparing me for our trip to visit her family.

"My dad is very... earnest in his prayers. No pun intended." She looked at me and grinned (her father's name is Ernest). "I love prayer, don't get me wrong.. I just prefer prayer that is short and to the point when it comes to praying over my meal. For example, this one time when I was about 14, I had just recently bought a new wrist watch that had a timer option on it, it was so cool... Or at least it was cool to me."

She shrugged with a little laugh. "Anyhow, most my family and I were all seated around the dinner table waiting for my dad to finish washing up when I decided I wanted to see how long my dad's prayer would be. He sits down and we all bow our heads in prayer, right? Well, as soon as my dad began, I started the clock. I kid you not- the prayer lasted 9 minutes and 54 seconds." She starts to laugh as she catches her breath.

By this point I'm laughing. Feeling intrigued I asked, "What is it your dad prays about that makes his prayers for the meal last so long?"

She laughed out loud to my question and simply states "Everything." Seeing that I am looking for more of an explanation she continued, " He prays over the food, for someone he may have seen that day, individual family members, different farm problems, needs or blessings, a prayer request he heard at church or possibly from someone, an upcoming marriage, for the family of someone who may have just died and then he'll pray over the food again. And just as he is normally about to say 'Amen' he remembers something else and begins praying about that as well." She couldn't help but to smile as she described the humor she found in his prayer. "My mom just learned to keep the food covered until he says his final 'Amen'."

As Mr. Sutton finally closed in prayer and I glanced at Larissa and squeezed her hand before letting go.

As we ate, the conversation went well. Mr. Sutton was eager to hear about our farm in Lancaster County, and my dad was more than happy to talk about it, as always. As we continued to visit, I could see how her sisters were watching me closely. I could tell they were very skeptical about me and I was sure it was because they had heard about our first date. They were watching me closely to determine if I was dangerously bad news, or just intensely romantic and out of my mind.

Her dad, on the other hand, didn't seem to question anything at all. So far, my initial meeting with him was going very well. It was almost going too well, in fact. It was very clear he had no idea about our first date at all. Now I was conflicted about whether I should tell him or not. Traditionally, this was an "ask the dad permission to court his daugher" kind of household. A standard I had clearly bypassed. That fact didn't seem to bother him at this point, as he seemed genuinely interested in getting to know me and my background. With how well our families were getting along, I certainly didn't want to ruin a good thing by abruptly mentioning our first date. At least not yet.

As the weekend continued, our visit was going better than I could have hoped for. I helped milk cows in the barn in the evening, then helped clean manure out of the gutters. Their milking system was more old fashioned than I had ever seen. It was even older than the barn my family used when I was a child, before they updated to a new barn. Now they have a modern milking parlor enabling them to milk 24 cows at a time, with a herd of 450. My dad pioneered the construction of this barn when I was in elementary school. The Sutton's farm at least had a vacuum pump system to get the milk out, but they still had to manually carry the buckets of milk by hand and dump it into the tank. I had never seen anybody work so hard to milk only 32 cows.

Once the milking was done, the gutters were full of manure. We used shovels and a wheelbarrow to transport the manure over to the manure spreader. This was certainly an old way of doing things. For the most part, my family's farm has an automatic system to clean the manure. As we worked, all of the stories Larissa had told me about her childhood began to have more of a clear picture in my mind.

Everything she had said was spot on about how they did things here. She'd told me about how long the chores lasted, which explained why her and her sisters were typically stronger than any of the other girls they knew. She described how the animals were all practically pets due to each and every one of them having nicknames and being treated with such care. Everyone had their separate chores or responsibilities to tend to.

We were all laughing or telling stories while we worked together, pitching in to help each other with their work so we could get everything done sooner. The work was incredibly hard, yet rewarding.

After a morning session of cleaning gutters in the barn, I stood outside the front door to the house discussing with Larissa whether or not I should tell her dad about our first date. I stood directly face-to-face with her as I interlocked my fingers behind her neck, resting my forearms on her shoulders, while leaving enough space for Jesus between us. As Larissa and I were in our discussion, Mr. Sutton peeked his head out of the milk-house and called out: "Save the best for later!" The distance we had between us didn't appear to be enough from his point of view. He didn't sound angry at all, but wanted to make sure we were watching our physical boundaries. Larissa jumped back as I dropped my arms away from her as we both looked back at him replied "Okay!"

"Thank you!" he said as he smiled and waved, stepping back into the milk-house. Larissa and I looked at each other and laughed awkwardly about having to be reprimanded for something we didn't realize or think was "crossing the line". Of course we were going to be saving sex for marriage, but the idea of not being able to even have my hands on her shoulders was foreign to me.

After all the work was done in the barn, the Suttons took us on a hike to some nearby waterfalls so we could see more of their hometown. My parents were getting along with them incredibly well, just as I expected they would. So far, everything was going according to plan.

Meanwhile, in the duration of the weekend, I had an internal battle I was dealing with. If Mr. Sutton had no idea about the first date, should I tell him? And when would be a good time? And how should I tell him? Mrs. Sutton had dropped comments here and there about it, making it clear she was aware. The entire family was just as nervous as Larissa was about how he would react to it. They were beginning to like me and were feeling concerned this might put me in low regard with Mr. Sutton. I felt confident I could explain it to him in a way that he would be understanding. I didn't think it would go over very well if I decided not to tell him and he heard about it from someone else. I discussed this with Larissa and her mom. Larissa was afraid of how he would react and didn't think I should tell him yet. Mrs. Sutton held the middle ground and didn't push me one way or the other. I ultimately decided that telling him about it was something I needed to do. It just came down to finding the right moment.

The day we were preparing to leave, Mr. Sutton was sitting in the living room across from my parents as they were visiting. If I was going to tell him about the first date, I wasn't going to find a better time than this moment. My parents were there to back me up and if things went sour, and we would be leaving soon anyway. Larissa hung out in the kitchen where she could still hear everything since she knew what was coming and she did not want to be in the room when her dad found out. She was very pessimistic about the potential outcome of the conversation.

After a few minutes of participating in aimless conversation with my parents and Mr. Sutton, I went right into it. "Hey Mr. Sutton, I hope you know that I think your daughter is really awesome," I began. "In fact, the day after Larissa and I met we were texting and she had told me to prepare for her awesomeness to return to Lancaster, and I had told her to watch out, because I'm the most awesome thing to happen to Lancaster. She then told me that I might be the most awesome thing to happen to Lancaster, but she was the most 'awesomest thing that God put on the planet.'"

"That sounds like something she would claim." Mr. Sutton nodded and laughed with delight as I began my bold explanation.

So far he thought this was pretty funny. I continued with my story, speaking with as much confidence as when Bobby interrogated me. "In fact, when she told me that, I couldn't help but take her seriously. I was initially able to get her to agree to go out to eat. At the time, Larissa was thinking this would be as friends, but I was considering it to be a date. And the more I thought about it, the less sense it made to take the most awesome girl in the world out on a date as if she was just an ordinary girl. I felt like it made more sense to take her out on the most awesomest date in the world."

Mr. Sutton continued to listen intently as he was still smiling and enjoying my story. At this point there was no turning back. My parents sat and listened as I shared the story they knew quite well by now. They still enjoyed hearing it, and of course I enjoyed telling it. (I was quite good at it by this time, as I would tell the story any chance I had.)

"So when I was thinking about where I should take her on a date, I came up with the the idea of taking her to California for a weekend. I talked to her about joining me for a weekend with some friends and she agreed. Since she loves surprises so much, I didn't tell her what the plan was, so she had no idea where we were going. I looked online and found some great deals for airline tickets, so I bought them and reserved the rental car."

At this point it looked like his eyes were so wide it appeared as though they were ready to pop out of his head. His mouth was agape as he processed what I was telling him. As an older, conservative man, this was the most outrageous thing he could have possibly expected to hear. Before he started jumping to conclusions and thinking the worst of me I needed to immediately offer him some assurance.

"Honestly, I wouldn't have been comfortable taking her to a place I didn't know anybody or I hadn't been before, but I lived in Los Angeles for a year and I have several friends living there. To me, it's like a second home. My friends provided separate sleeping arrangements and I offered to get her a hotel room of her own if that made her more comfortable."

My parents chimed in as they could see Mr. Sutton becoming so dismayed he couldn't assemble any words to express his reaction. "I can promise you I have no doubt in my mind that Tom and Larissa didn't do anything inappropriate while they were over there. Tom is a good guy and he is very adventurous and I know it sounds very crazy, but that's just who he is.

We can assure you he want about this very appropriately." *Yes. That's why. That's why my parents were there.*

I continued with my explanation. "To me, the greatest thing about this trip was that I had the opportunity to take Larissa to all my favorite places from when I lived out there. I was able to take her climbing where I used to rock climb, I was able to show her the town I used to live, and I even showed her the house I called home. My life in LA is a big part of who I am, and it meant a lot that I was able to share that part of me with her. Now when I talk about those places she can put herself there and envision what I'm talking about. The same way my visit here gives me a better idea of where she grew up, I can now picture things better when she tells me stories from her past." I stated as I concluded with my story.

All of this was true as well. Larissa really was special. It was truly wonderful that I was able to share this part of me with her. The first date was more than a simple adventure. She seemed special enough that I wanted her to know that part of who I am.

The expression on Mr. Sutton's face still hadn't changed. Wide eyed and mouth agape. In the meantime, Larissa was cringing in the kitchen as she knew the exact expression he was making.

"Well." Mr. Sutton finally spoke up, after my long-winded explanation. "That is really quite a story." He said with serious amusement. He wasn't necessarily excited about my story, but he wasn't upset either. He could tell I was genuine in my explanation, and my parents were there backing me up as well. "If you ever do something crazy like this again, just be sure to let me know ahead of time." He stated with just a bit of subtle laughter. The smile on his face as was beginning to show he felt reassured about the whole situation. I nailed it. Mission accomplished. I probably couldn't have pitched my story better to him.

Now I knew I was going to have to tell him about the next trip that was already set in stone. Of course it was too soon to tell him, but I knew I needed to inform him about it one way or another before it happened. "Let me give you my blessing." He said to me. He stood up from his chair and walked over to me. He put his hand on my shoulder, smiled, and nodded.

I wasn't sure how the blessing thing worked, but I was at least in good standings with him. I felt good. Not only did I have a clear conscious after telling him about the first date, but I received his blessing over our relationship immediately afterwards. It was a solid day of winning. Winning is something I never get tired of. And now I had more winning to do. I needed to win over his approval to marry her in a relatively short amount of time. So far I knew I was off to a great start.

Mr. Sutton gave me a book to read called "Man in the Mirror." Now I had homework to do. Easy enough. I would make sure to read the book cover to cover and be ready to hand it back to him the next time we were there to visit.

As our weekend was coming to an end, I was thankful for the opportunity to get to know more of Larissa's family, and leave a good impression upon them. Larissa, my parents and I climbed into the van, and prepared for a long drive home. Larissa's parents waved us off as we left, standing outside to watch us go. They waved us goodbye until we were out of the driveway and on our way down the road. We made ourselves comfortable as my parents took another unnecessarily long detour to get us back home to Lancaster.

CHAPTER 8
One More Red Flag

I t was mid summer and our relationship was continuing to progress at an accelerated pace. Now that we'd been together for a few months and received a blessing on our relationship, we decided it was time to talk to Bobby and get him on board with the fake eloping trip. It would not only be a lot of fun to have him join us for such a trip, but if he was a part of it, we could still be in good graces with their family by the time all was said and done.

At this point, the family knew our relationship was more than likely a permanent thing, and Bobby still held me in high regard. Larissa and Bobby were always close growing up, and continued to stay in close contact. Fortunately, because of their connection, Larissa and I were able to maintain an open line of communication with him. This allowed him to remain confident in me as a person, and the relationship I had with Larissa.

Larissa and I called him up and explained our plan to fake elope. We went over the details of finding an Elvis in Las Vegas, having Larissa in a white dress and me in a suit to make it look as if we had eloped by posting photos of us all over social media. We explained following the fake elopement, we would be going to Los Angeles followed by a trip up the coast and a couple days in Sacramento. Of course it was an outrageous idea, but we knew Bobby would be up for it.

"That sounds like a crazy idea," Bobby responded to our proposition, "but I'm totally game. I've always wanted to go to California and this sounds like it's going to be an awesome prank. So I'm totally in!" He was enthusiastic and supportive. I couldn't believe everything was coming together so flawlessly.

My next potential obstacle to overcome was to get a blessing from Mr. Sutton so I could ask for his daughter's hand in marriage. The next time I was going to be seeing him was when Larissa and I would be going to New York for her sister's wedding in early September. If he told me "No" or to wait, that would certainly put a serious wrench into my plans.

Another brilliant idea I had come up with was to get Larissa's best friend Cara to join us. Surely it would add a fun element to the trip if Larissa had a girl to accompany her on this adventure. Rather than being just her and 3 guys. I figured it would be fun if Larissa was unaware of Cara joining us, so she could surprise Larissa when we landed in Vegas. I knew I had to be as vague as possible when I brought this idea up to her, in case it didn't work for her to join us. If she wasn't able to go, I would still want her to believe, just like everybody else, that Larissa and I had legitimately eloped.

I called her up and cautiously began the conversation. "Hey Cara, before I start, I need to know that you promise not to tell anyone anything about this conversation."

"Ok, I won't tell anyone." She said. I could hear a smile behind her voice. She was a serious advocate for my relationship with Larissa. She loved the fact that I had whisked her away to California for our first date, and knew from the beginning that Larissa and I were perfect for each other. I was sure she knew this secret conversation we were having had something to do with my plan to propose to Larissa.

"I have something huge I want to involve you in, but I can't tell you any details right now. I'll first tell you the time it's going to take and how much money it will cost. If you can handle both of those, I'll tell you what the plan is, and you can decide if it's worth it, which I know it definitely is. But I can't tell you anything unless you're available to be part of it. Alright?"

"Sounds like a deal to me." She responded. I knew I had certainly piqued her interest at this point, and I was really hoping this could work. Especially since it would make the trip all the more special for Larissa. This way she wouldn't be the only girl on the trip, and her best friend could witness the proposal. Additionally, I knew Cara was an incredible photographer. If she was along with us, she could take engagement photos of us as we traveled along the coast in some of the most beautiful places in the country. She would really add a lot of value to this trip and I was really hoping this could work.

"I would need you to be free on September 21 through the 25th, and it would cost you right around $300 for everything." (I was figuring on paying for the car rental and lodging. Besides that, she would only have to pay for her airline ticket and food. I was generous, but not rich.)

"It sounds like you have an awesome plan of some kind, but I have classes happening that I shouldn't skip, and it's a little short notice. I'm not sure if I'd be able to come up with the money, since I'd have to also save up for the work I would be missing. I really wish I could join you, but I can't." She sounded disappointed. "I hope things come together for you, though!"

"No worries at all. I totally understand." I told her. "Just forget this conversation ever happened and don't tell anybody."

I was pretty disappointed she wouldn't be able to join us, but I couldn't hold it against her. I was sure if there was any possibility she could make it work, she would have.

During this time, I had also discovered I managed to schedule this to happen on a weekend I was supposed to work on the farm. Typically I would rotate every other weekend off with one of the farm's hired hands. Not only was I needed for the day-to-day operations on the Saturdays, but I was expected to milk cows on Sunday afternoons as well. I only had to milk one Sunday afternoon every 4 weeks as a rotation with other employees, but I had been a little short-sighted to overlook this factor in my plans. Surely if God wanted this to happen, He would allow there to be a way. I knew what I was up against to get my Saturday off. The specific worker I would need to trade with was always quite adamant about sticking to his schedule. Fortunately, he approached me asking if I could work his Saturday for an event he was attending with his wife and kids in July. I was quick to agree, as long as he took my place so I could have off on my birthday weekend. He happily agreed to it since it worked for both of us.

I talked with one of the girls who milked cows in the parlor. I asked if she could secretly take my place milking on the Sunday afternoon while I would be gone. I told her she wasn't allowed to tell anyone about it and she would just show up to help. She was happy to agree to it and promised not to tell anyone about it ahead of time.

I felt relieved to have these things lined up and figured out. Everything was lining up just about perfectly right up until I got a text from Glenda a few weeks later. Apparently, she wasn't as free on the dates I had given her as she had initially thought. She told me we were welcome to stay at her place, but she had a lot of work happening and she wouldn't be able to spend much time with us. That was a huge disappointment as I was looking forward to visiting with her, but it wasn't necessarily anything that made it impossible for us to visit or do this trip.

The next problem that arose was a bit more difficult to solve. Our hired hand approached me in the barn and told me his family's plans had changed and they would no longer be going away that weekend in July, so he wouldn't need to switch weekends with me after all. I told him that I would still need the time off for my birthday weekend since I had made some big plans. He countered that he would be doing something for his wife's birthday that weekend and could not oblige, with a "not-my-problem" attitude.

Now I would not only be expected at work, but by leaving when I had planned, I would be giving everybody on the farm an additional workload to cover. They would notice I was missing as soon as I failed to show up for work on Saturday, instead of discovering on Sunday that I had fled to Vegas with Larissa, giving them adequate time to make arrangements to get work done on Monday. This wasn't good. I wasn't comfortable with bailing on work. I didn't want to have to ask off since I knew my family couldn't help but be curious why I would need the time off. Any time-off required an un-official explanation. Refusing to give an explanation would lead to assumptions, and rumors to spread around the farm. Since I was in a relationship they were confident would end up in marriage, they would not only want to hear why I wanted off work, but they would be jumping to conclusions. The last thing I needed was my sister to get excited and suggest to Larissa that I might be proposing to her. I had been doing everything I could to keep the thought from entering her head and a proposal was the last inkling I wanted to be planted into her mind. I knew it wasn't an option to go that route. It would most likely mess up my entire plan.

I was also up against another issue: The corn harvest. Typically we would finish harvesting early in September, but the weather had prevented us from planting the corn as early as we typically would. This was shaping us up for a harvest that would likely happen on the weekend Larissa and I would be in Las Vegas "fake eloping." I knew this would certainly strip any potential humor or joy out of it for my family, even though we would be coming home engaged. They would never forgive me for doing such a thing, either. My plan to do this trip at a convenient time for the sake of the farm and everyone else involved was quickly falling apart.

Now I had some serious things to ponder. One sunny day, I was out trimming weeds around the electric fence with a machete. This task needed to be done at least once a year to keep the electric in the fence from shorting out. As I walked along the meadow hacking away at the weeds, I was deep in thought. I knew this was the girl God wanted me to spend the rest of my life with, but why were things not coming together very well? Should I change the date for the trip? I hated the idea of inconveniencing Bobby, since he already agreed to take the time off from work to join us for this venture. I really didn't want to make things difficult for him, as I felt as though his schedule and all of our plans were set in stone, and the last thing I wanted to do was mess with his schedule. Not to mention the fact that I would have to reschedule the flights for me, Larissa, and Cameron. I knew that wouldn't be cheap, either. As much as I wanted to push through this and past the numerous barriers being placed in my way, there was no denying how difficult this plan was becoming.

As I used the machete as a form of stress relief, hacking away at weeds in the sunlight with sweat running down my face and body, I prayed to God. "God." I began. "I trust that you are in control of all aspects of my life. Thank you for the awesome relationship I have with Larissa. You know that things aren't coming together quite perfectly for this fake elopement. I pray that if you want me to post-pone this, if you want me to push it back and do it at another time, just give me one more red flag. Just give me one more reason to push it back and I will."

After I finished going around the meadow fence and the sun had set, wrapping up my day, I spent the evening with Larissa at my place. We were in the middle of watching a movie when her phone rang. It was Bobby. She picked it up and they spent a few minutes catching up. Then he had something he wanted to share with both of us. Larissa put the phone on speaker. "Hey guys," he began "so I was really want-ing to do this whole fake eloping thing with you. I love the idea, and it sounds like it would be a lot of fun, but I feel like God wants me to speak at an event at Fairwood, and it would be the same time as the trip."

I could tell he loathed bringing this news to us. He had probably been putting it off as long as he could. " I can't express to you how disappointed I am. I've always wanted go to California, and I was really excited about this trip, but it's just not going to work for me. I'm really sorry."

Boom. There it was. Another red flag. I didn't even have to second guess it. "Okay, well, would you want to go in December instead?" I asked so casually without any hesitation. Now I knew God wanted us to postpone this. Not only was it another red flag, but it was the perfect red flag. Bobby's schedule was my biggest concern when it came to rescheduling our trip. The fact that Bobby came to us was clearly God's answer to my prayer.

"Yeah." Bobby responded, sounding pleased and surprised at how easy it was for me to accept his sudden change in plans. "I would love to go in December. Could you shoot me some dates so I can ask off work and look into some flights?"

"Absolutely." I responded. "I'll find a date that works for us and I'll run it by you before I change our flight plans." We enthusiastically ended the conversation with Bobby so we could start getting some plans together.

Larissa and I spent the rest of the evening looking over flights and working on revisions for our trip. We called Glenda to discuss the changes with her and find out what dates in December would work well for her, now that our plans were more flexible. It turned out she had some time off early in the month that would give her plenty of time to spend with us. Additionally, she had already planned a birthday celebration for her daughter, Taylor during that time. As long as we stayed on schedule, we would be able to join them for the surprise party. Changing our travel plans was already working seamlessly.

Since we would be going in December, there wouldn't be any work to be done in the fields, so the farm wouldn't be nearly as busy. If I was gone, there was still plenty of help to get the necessary work done. Since we were going to be rescheduling our flights, we decided to add a day to the trip so we could have an extra day to take it easy at Glenda's. We were on a tight itinerary through the entire trip, and an extra day at Glenda's to recuperate would take a lot of stress out of the adventure. Not to mention, we would have more time to spend with Glenda, Taylor and Trevor.

We concluded that we would leave December 7th and be flying back December 12th. I was scheduled to have the weekend off on the farm, so I wouldn't be dependant on anyone to switch their schedule with me. We found some flights that worked well and matched the price we had already paid.

I gave Cameron a call to give him a rundown on the situation. I told him I would absorb the cost of changing his flight, since I was the one initiating the change. He told me the new dates for the trip worked just as well and he would get the time off.

Before locking them in, we reviewed the dates with Bobby so he could make sure it would suit his schedule. He told us he would look into it immediately and get back to us soon.

After all of our planning and research, it was getting late and Larissa needed to go home and get to sleep, since she had work early the next morning. She headed out the door and immediately after she left I called Bobby again. I went on to tell him about how I had prayed to God earlier in the day, and how his call was a direct answer to prayer. I explained the ultimate reasoning behind the trip was to propose to Larissa while we were in California. I told him I was intending to ask their dad for his blessing, and I wanted to get a blessing from him as well, but it wasn't a conversation I wanted to have over the phone.

Bobby admitted he had a suspicion that was the real purpose of the trip, and agreed that we would talk in person when we were in New York for Katie's wedding in September. Since God pushed back the timing for the proposal, I decided I wouldn't be asking Larissa's father for his blessing to marry her this trip. I trusted God to give me the opportunity to ask for a blessing on another occasion before December. This would give us time to further display our maturing relationship to her family, without making it seem as though we were rushing things too much.

Within the next week, Bobby had agreed on the definitive date. Cameron was able to change the dates he had asked off for work as well, so we were all set. I called the airline to change our itinerary. It wasn't a cheap process, but I knew it was what needed to be done.

Now that we had some definitive dates further into the future, I decided to check with Cara again. I called her up with the same approach. "Okay. There've been a few changes and I have the same deal for you. This would now happen December 7th-12th. If you can manage the time off and about $300 in costs, let me know. I'll tell you what the plan is and you can decide if you want to be a part of it, which I know you will."

"Okay, let me look at my schedule here." Cara responded. I knew if it was at all possible for her to make it, she would. "It looks like I actually don't have any classes that week. And the family I nanny for is going to be on vacation, so I don't even have any work to miss out on. I don't have the money on hand right now, but I will later. So I'm in. What's the plan?"

I explained the idea for fake eloping, my plan to propose to Larissa in Los Angeles, and the trip up the coast and the time in Sacramento. I told her I would be providing the rental car and the lodging. I was sure to inform her of the fact that Larissa had no idea I was talking to her about this trip and she wouldn't have any clue she would be a part of this. I mentioned that if it helped, I would be able to reserve her airline ticket and she could just pay me back later. I also suggested to her about how this could also be a great opportunity for her to take some phenomenal photos and expand her photography portfolio.

"That sounds like an awesome plan! I'm totally game! I could get a lot of good photos while we're out there. Especially if we're going to be traveling up the coast. We could probably find some sweet places to take your engagement photos!"

"That's exactly what I was thinking! Sounds, awesome. I'm so excited for this!" I said. "I'll get in touch with you when I find the right flights, and I'll find a good time to call you while I reserve them, so I can get the information I need."

I couldn't be more excited. I loved the idea of having Cara with us. Not because of the photo's she could take, but in a way, she would complete the group. She'd be there to see her best friend become engaged. She'd be the one to squeal in excitement with Larissa in their hotel room. Larissa didn't have to feel alone in any way during one of the most life-changing nights of her life.

Within a few days I found some well priced flights from Manchester, New Hampshire to Las Vegas, Nevada. I called her and she confirmed the dates. She gave me the info I needed as I ordered the tickets. She was locked in.

There I was with a very elaborate plan in motion. Larissa, Cameron and I would fly out of Baltimore, Bobby would fly out of Atlanta, and Cara would fly out of Manchester. We would all be meeting up in Las Vegas to pull of the most epic prank of our lives. Larissa was completely oblivious about Cara being a part of this plan, so I was looking forward to seeing her reaction to such a surprise. Now we had several months of anticipation with a large secret we couldn't share with anyone.

In September, when Larissa and I went to New York for her sister Katie's wedding, this was my first opportunity to meet several of her siblings and start building relationships. Additionally, I would be able to spend more time with Bobby. It was only the second time I had a chance to get together with him and would be the last until we saw each other in Las Vegas.

One evening, Bobby and I went out to eat pizza at one of his favorite local places, giving us an excellent opportunity to talk. We talked about our anticipation of the trip out west, how crazy it was all going to be, and how much fun we were going to have. We then discussed my relationship with Larissa. Bobby spoke fondly of her and mentioned how pleased he was with our relationship. I took advantage of the moment and asked him if I had his blessing to propose to Larissa. As much as Larissa looked up to him, I felt asking for his blessing would be an honorable thing to do.

Bobby was happy to give me his blessing, which was incredibly meaningful to receive. He said with my ambition, sense of adventure, and my crazy antics, I was just right for her. He was looking forward to seeing how things progressed with our relationship, and he was very supportive of the idea of eventually becoming my brother in law.

After spending a full, long weekend in New York, we drove home to Pennsylvania. I had three long months until I was going to propose, and at some point in between, I needed to make one more trip back up to ask her father an important question.

Time flew by much faster than I thought it would. Before I knew it, we were well into the month of November and I still hadn't had a chance to get up to New York to ask Larissa's dad for his blessing. Not getting his blessing to marry his daughter was simply not an option. I pondered the idea of going up to Boston with my friend Jason, primarily so we could swing by her parent's house in New York to get his blessing, but I felt like it would be impossible to do so without Larissa finding out about it from one of her sisters. I was running out of time and options.

"I think we should go visit your family again sometime soon." I said to Larissa one day. Her eyes widened and looked incredibly confused and disappointed at the same time. She was enjoying her independence in Lancaster and didn't like the idea of visiting the farm she had escaped from.

"But.. I don't want to." She pleaded. "Why do you feel like we need to go up there?" Obviously it was going to be very difficult to convince Larissa why we should randomly go visit her family.

"Well, we spend all of our time here, and my family has had the chance to get to know you very well. They see you almost every day. I've only been up to visit your family twice, and they really haven't had much of a chance to get to know me. I think it would be best if I had the chance to visit them on at least 10 separate occasions before I ask your dad for his blessing for us to get married, someday." After I told her this, her face looked as disappointed as a three year old who was just told there was no Santa Claus. She believed every word I just told her, and it was exactly what I wanted. After all, there was some sense to what I was saying. Her dad certainly wouldn't hand her off to a guy he barely knew, would he?

To Larissa, the fake elopement was just that. A fake elopement. To her, there was no larger reason, or explanation to why we were going out west. I was thankful her heart was so set on playing such a large, elaborate joke.

"I guess we can go. If we have to." She said with a sigh as she pushed out her lower lip far enough for me to see she was pouting. Had she known the real reason I wanted to go to New York, she would have been as excited as a kid on Christmas morning.

That weekend we headed up to her family's farm. It was literally the last weekend I would have the chance to go before the fake elopement. Larissa had absolutely no enthusiasm, whatsoever, toward what seemed to be an unnecessary trip to the farm. Regardless, if my intention was to visit her family on ten separate occasions, she figured we may as well go to New York every chance I was feeling inspired to.

When the weekend for our visit finally approached, after a solid five hour drive, we arrived at her family's farm. We arrived in time to enjoy dinner with the family, which was followed by singing hymns around the table. The next day was filled with the usual chores. They milked in the morning and I came out to help finish and clean gutters. We sent the cows back out to the meadow and at some point during the day, they got out and we had to run down the road to chase them back to where they belonged. Apparently the cows manage to get out often. (Larissa had told me stories about having to often chase cows back into the meadow when she was growing up.)

All day I was looking for an opportunity to speak with Mr. Sutton one-on-one so I could ask for his daughter's hand in marriage. I didn't even know how I was going to ask. I didn't know what I was going to say, and I certainly didn't know how he would respond, either. I knew I was in good standing with him, but he hadn't had a whole lot of opportunity to get to know me very well. Ever since I had received Bobby's blessing, Bobby had spoken to Mr. Sutton every so often and made sure to speak well of me so he could help improve my odds.

I felt I had a really solid chance to receive a blessing, though I knew that things were going to be really awkward if he said no. I wasn't sure how I would react to that. The best that I could do was pray that he would say yes, and pray for a good opportunity to talk to him.

By Saturday evening I still hadn't found the right time to bring this conversation to Mr. Sutton, and Larissa and I were going to head back to Pennsylvania the next day. I continually prayed for the opportunity to talk to Mr. Sutton, and I grew increasingly nervous that it might not present itself. Larissa and I were in the living room with the family and Mr. Sutton suddenly decided he needed to go check on the pipeline washer in the barn. The system was recently installed so they wouldn't have to carry the milk by hand to the tank, but the washer system still had some kinks to be worked out and didn't always work properly.

"I'll go with you" I said, as I excused myself to go help him. Here it was. My opportunity to ask for his blessing.

I walked into the milk house with Mr. Sutton and the washer system was running. He wanted to stay and see it go through a cycle to be sure it was doing it's job properly. This was a good opportunity for us to talk, even though the muffler for the washer system screamed as we talked over it. I don't even remember what we started our conversation with, but after making some small talk, I decided to seize the moment go for it.

"So what do you think of me and your daughter by now?" I began, doing my best to casually steer the conversation toward me and Larissa.

"Well," he began as he smiled. "I think you're certainly a fine gentleman. You seem to really love the Lord and respect my daughter very well. I know you've spent some time with Bobby and he speaks very highly of you." He said in his cheerful voice. I was about to tell him that I appreciated hearing that, but he continued on. "So I guess you're here to ask for my daughter's hand in marriage?" He inquired with a smile.

Wow, that certainly makes it easy, I thought to myself, finding humor in how easy he was making this for me. I spoke up in response to his wise assumption "Yes, I actually would like to ask for her hand in marriage."

"Well I think you're certainly the right guy for her. You love the Lord and I've never seen her so happy with anybody. You really are made for each other and I can see that. You do have my blessing." He said as he made this conversation incredibly easier than I could have ever asked for.

As we walked out of the milk house and into the stall barn I happened to recall how he told me that if I was doing anything crazy again that I should let him know first. I debated in my mind if I should really tell him about my plan for the fake elopement and how I was going to propose. I felt as though the concept of fake eloping might push the envelope for him just a little too much, so I figured I should be as vague as possible.

"Remember how you wanted me to tell you if I was going to do anything crazy again like the first date?" I asked him as I prepared to inform him I would be taking his daughter across the country again.

"I do. Why do you ask?" He inquired as he could sense I was going to have another plan up my sleeve.

"Well, I do want you to know there's a place in California that I want to propose to her, but for this trip, Bobby, Cameron and Cara are going to be joining us." I told him. He seemed to be quite intrigued with this concept. Since Bobby was going to be a part of it, he felt assured about the thought of me taking Larissa across the country again.

Since I didn't want to startle him with the crazy idea of fake eloping, I continued on doing my best to make sure he would clearly understand me. "We will be doing this trip on December 7th." Before continuing, I made direct eye contact and said to him with a serious look on my face. "Just be sure not to believe anything you hear until you hear it directly from us." I stated this, trying to be as clear as possible while doing my best to be vague at the same time.

"Ok. Well, I wish you the best and I look forward to hearing about it later." He said with some laughter as we walked back toward the house.

This conversation couldn't have gone better. The final piece of the puzzle had come together and we were all set. The next morning Larissa and I drove back to Pennsylvania. We were two weeks away from a life-changing adventure and the time was quickly approaching.

CHAPTER 9
The Fake Elopement

At 9:00 A.M on the Saturday morning of December 7th, 2013 I woke up refreshed, yet feeling slightly intimidated by the audacious plan I had put in motion for the next few days. I had done my best to stay up late and sleep in as long as I could in efforts to shift my sleeping schedule to Pacific Standard Time. Since my mother was under the impression Larissa and I had nothing going on that day, she convinced Larissa to wake up early and go to a Christmas Crafts Show happening in town. Larissa wanted to sleep in just like I did, especially since she was beginning to feel sick, but felt obligated to go the craft show since we told her we had no other plans for the day. Larissa couldn't come up with any valid excuses and wasn't sick enough to talk her way out of it.

I didn't manage to sleep in quite as long as I was hoping, but after getting out of bed, I grabbed a quick breakfast and started packing my bag immediately after. As I packed my best suit, along with clothes appropriate for California weather, I did my best to hide the ring I had purchased for

Larissa in a place there was absolutely no chance she would find it.

After I finished packing, I headed out to pick up Cameron. He did a great job of not telling his parents anything about what our plan was, just as I had requested. This was a top secret mission and I didn't want to leave anything to chance. Cameron and I snuck his bag into my car then headed upstairs to casually talk to his parents. Naturally, they were asking us about our plans for the day, as any curious parent would. We just shrugged it off and told them we really didn't have anything specific in mind. I'm not fond of lying to people, especially a friend's parents, but for as much as I hated to do so, I wasn't willing to jeopardize my plan.

Cameron and I got in the car and headed back to my house. Larissa arrived a few minutes after we did with the bag she had smuggled out of her place and into her car. She talked about how my mom was so nice to her all morning and bought her a pair of earrings from the Christmas craft show they attended. She told me about how guilt-ridden she'd been feeling all morning about having to hide the truth from my mom about our later flight to Las Vegas.

Everything was starting to feel surreal. The plan we had assembled was a lot of fun to talk about, but now we were actually going to do this. I felt as though I had to shut out all my nervous feelings about this outrageous thing we were going to do and numbingly force myself to trust my instincts and go through with it. Who does something this crazy? This was certainly more absurd than what any normal person would think to put themselves up to. Fortunately, I'm far from normal.

While Larissa, Cameron and I were in my kitchen grabbing a quick bite to eat, Cameron chimed into the conversation. "You know" he started, "I'd really like to thank you guys for including me in the most expensive prank ever." Larissa and I laughed at his comment. He always had a funny way of looking at things. He knew my full plan was to propose to Larissa, but regardless, this *was* an expensive prank. To Larissa, there was no better way to explain it. I knew this was going to be well worth it. Especially if I came back with a fiance.

We snuck my bags out to the car, making sure nobody on the farm would happen to be driving past and question where we were going. It was difficult to keep secrets on the farm, and word travels much faster than an Allis Chalmers tractor. The car was loaded and we were ready to go by 2PM, giving us plenty of time for anything to possibly go wrong. Since we couldn't come up with anything better, or more logical to do, we decided we would drive to the airport and be extra early for our flight, which was scheduled to depart at 7:45.

We had about an hour and a half drive ahead of us. We would be parking my car at a hotel and taking a shuttle to the airport. As I was driving, Larissa paged through the papers I had printed out for the long term parking, airline tickets, and rental car.

"You rented a MINIVAN?!!" She exclaimed as she looked closely at the paperwork for the rental. She was absolutely disgusted. "You know how much I hate minivans. We're going to be cruising around California looking really stupid. We don't even need one."

"Well, there is going to be five of us..." Cameron blurted out.

"No," I said, as I nonchalantly glared at him in the back-seat. "There's only four of us. Me, you, Larissa and Bobby."

"Oh, that's right." He said as he remembered that Larissa was still unaware of Cara's involvement on the trip. " I guess that is only four..." He stated with a subtly sarcastic tone.

"But Tom, why would you rent a minivan? It's not even necessary!" She continued on in her frustration.

"I figured it would give us plenty of extra space so we wouldn't be cramped in a car with all the driving we would be doing."

"I'd rather be cramped in a car than to be caught in a minivan." She responded.

"Well, when we get to the car rental place, we can look into the option of changing the reservation." I told her. I knew once she found out Cara would be joining us she would understand why I rented a minivan. For now, it was fun see-ing how much she loathed the idea of being seen in one.

I knew Larissa wasn't legitimately upset with me. Since she grew up in a household of snarky remarks and witty come-backs, she was never afraid to tell anyone how she really felt, or lay down a serious burn. She knew that I knew full well that she had no intention of ever driving or owning a mini-van, and her natural instinct was to give me trouble about it.

When we arrived at the hotel where we'd be leaving the car, I went to the front desk and collected the paper I would be placing in my windshield. We were all set, and if felt good to be at the airport with time to spare. We grabbed our bags and waited for the next shuttle.

Once we arrived at the airport, we checked our bags and breezed our way through security without any issues. Now we had a few hours to kill in the terminal. I felt it would be an excellent opportunity to film some short videos of our experience so we had more to share later. I asked Larissa about how she was feeling, while holding my camera up to her. "I feel okay right now." She responded. "I'm listening to music to try and calm my nerves."

"Why are you nervous?" I asked her rhetorically as I continued to film her priceless response. "Because we're about to fly to Las Vegas. It's kind of a scary thing to do when you haven't done it before." She said nervously. Then she went into a more detailed description of how she was feeling. "Planning this was a great idea. Like, legit, it hadn't been done before, kind of idea. Planning it was a lot of fun. It was really exciting. Now that we're in the process of working out those plans and actually doing it, it's kind of terrifying. The only way I can compare it, is when you go into the Army; you go through all kinds of training. You play military games and do strategic planning, preparing for war. You exercise all your plans and strategies playing in war games, like paintball, and it's awesome. It's fun! You roll around on the ground getting shot at, but then you actually go out to the war zone- where it's real. They ship you out, and it's really scary. 'Cause that's real. And the bullets are real. So this is a real bullet. I'm scared of people's reaction."

It *was* difficult to believe we were actually doing this. Now that we were in the terminal waiting for our plane to arrive, the reality was sinking in, and it was somewhat frightening.

"My dad is going to kill me. My family is going to hate me." Larissa said as her fears revealed themselves with our plans becoming reality with every passing minute.

I texted Cara and Bobby. Cara hadn't boarded her plane yet. Bobby was on his layover. An announcement came over our terminal that our flight had been overbooked and they were offering free flight vouchers to anyone willing to take a later flight. Given that Cara and Bobby would be waiting on us as it was, I couldn't go for it. Any other time I would have jumped on that offer in a heartbeat.

Our flight was coming in soon so it was time for me and Larissa to start stirring the pot. We took a selfie of us holding our airline tickets in front of us so people could clearly see we were flying to Las Vegas. We had large grins on our faces as though we were up to something. We each posted the photo to instagram and Facebook. We also posted a photo to our Snapchat story. Not even 10 minutes later Larissa received a text from Cara. "Girl, I don't know what's going on, but you had better call me and tell me! You are in trouble!" Cara was playing it off very well as though she had no idea what was going on.

"Oh man!" Larissa said. "Cara's mad! I feel so bad right now. I feel like such an awful person! I'm the worst best friend!"

"Just let it go. She'll get over it. We can just call her in a couple days and let her know it was just a prank." I assured Larissa. Meanwhile I sent Cara a text to let her know how well she had fooled Larissa.

Finally our flight came in and was ready to be boarded. We were scheduled to arrive in Las Vegas at 9:59, but our flight had been delayed and was already expecting to arrive half an hour late. We scanned our tickets and went to our seats. Larissa, Cameron and I were assigned seats all the way in the back. At first we thought it was going to be a great place to sit, without anyone to kick our chair behind us. Not long after we sat down did we realize how much it smelled like sewage, since we were so close to the restroom. (Not going to make that mistake again). Larissa, Cameron and I took a photo of the three of us and posted it to Instagram and Facebook with the statement "The cool kids in the back of the plane."

I sent Cara and Bobby a text letting them know our flight was taking off late. I also looked up their flight numbers and found they would be arriving on time. Bobby was expected to land not long after we were taking off. I shut my phone off and prepared for takeoff. Within a few short moments our plane was in the air. During the flight it seemed to become relatively turbulent and the pilot came over the loudspeaker to make an announcement. Our flight, which was already scheduled for a late arrival, would be arriving in Las Vegas an additional 45 minutes later since we would be facing a strong headwind the entire way there, slowing the plane down tremendously. This would be joyous for Cara and Bobby. At this pace they would be at the car rental facility for about an hour and a half before we arrived to meet them.

With the delays and anticipation, our already long flight felt as though it was taking an eternity to reach our destination. Once finally landed safely in Las Vegas and we were able turned our phones back on, we had some notifications from the photos we posted. We hadn't mentioned anything on them about eloping, but as I planned, people were already asking questions and jumping to conclusions. Then my phone buzzed with a voicemail. I put it to my ear and listened. It was my dad. He stated in a calm, yet authoritative tone "Tom, this is your father. I need you to call me right away. I would like to talk to you before you do something you might later regret. You have as all very worried here."

My gut was wrenching the same way it did when I was a child and knew I was in deep deep trouble. "Oh man, oh man, oh man!" I said. "My dad called me. He's really mad." I said to Larissa and Cameron. I wanted to call him and assure him everything was okay, but of course, I couldn't go back on what I told everybody else to do. My phone buzzed again with a text from my brother, Sam. "What the Hell, man?" it read. Wow. Sam never uses that word. I just took a deep breath and put my phone back in my pocket. Dealing with backlash wasn't a part of what I had imagined for this. It wasn't what I wanted. The thought of it was making my idea so much less fun. I had to let it go and allow it to roll off my back. The only way to experience any joy that hadn't yet been stripped out of the moment was to ignore the backlash and focus on accomplishing our mission. I trusted in the concept that when I would call my family after proposing to Larissa, everything would make sense to them and make it better. It was the only way I could push myself to go through with this and I needed to focus on the objective my family wasn't able to see at the time.

With every step I took towards the exit of the plane, the nervousness and anxiety from the voicemail slowly began to wear away. I needed to focus on our mission. Being in the back of the plane, it took us much longer than usual to get off. We eventually made it down to the baggage claim to get our luggage and wait for the bus that would transport us to the airport's car rental station. I looked at the time. It was 11pm, and we were running far behind our ideal schedule. Our late flight didn't help us at all.

The bus arrived after a few long minutes and we rode it to where we would be getting the rental car and meet up with Cara and Bobby.

We stepped off the bus and entered the facility. Looking around I could see every car rental company in existence. Enterprise, Budget, Hertz, Payless, and several others had their own kiosk. We looked around and found Bobby standing out in the open, waiting for us. We walked over to him feeling relieved to finally be together so we could execute this plan. I told Larissa to give her brother a big hug. She went forward to hug him awkwardly, given my unusual request. As soon as she leaned in for the hug, Cara ran around the corner with an exciting shriek and tackled Larissa in a big hug. At this moment I was hoping Larissa would get extremely excited and be blown away in excitement, but with the stress of our plan, the stress of traveling, and the stress of feeling somewhat sick already, she was more shocked than excited.

"What are you doing here?" She asked Cara very calmly though clearly confused and taken aback. "Somebody called me and told me you needed a bridesmaid!" Cara exclaimed with excitement. Larissa was still shocked. "That guy planned the whole thing." She said as she pointed to me.

"Holy crap! After I got your text I thought you were so mad at me!" Larissa exclaimed in laughter.

After we had a few moments of greeting each other, we needed to keep things rolling. It was after 11:00pm and we had a mission to accomplish. Bobby and I went to the kiosk to get the keys to the rental van and sign a few papers while Larissa and Cara visited. Once all the paperwork was complete we rushed out to the parking garage. Once we found the van, we loaded it up and piled in.

"Are you glad I have a van now?" I asked Larissa teasingly.

"Of course it makes sense now that I know there's five of us!" She happily responded. I could tell that having Cara there was certainly putting her at ease.

With Bobby and I in the front seat, Cara and Larissa in the middle, and Cameron chilling on the back bench, we were on our way. First and foremost, the most important thing we needed to do right away was go to In-N-Out Burger. I barely ate anything all day so I could enjoy the savory taste of a burger as though my life depended on it. Not to mention, Cameron had been craving it ever since we left California on our road trip a year and a half earlier. This would be the first time for Bobby and Cara to enjoy it.

After a joyous 20 minutes of eating our cheeseburgers and Double-Doubles, it was time to do what we set out to do. We piled into the van and drove to Fremont Street, where a friend told me we could probably find an Elvis impersonator. The street was vibrant with a cascade of lights to draw you in like a moth, as several casinos were lined up to give you several options to lose your money. Fremont Street was one of the largest tourist attractions in Las Vegas. We found a free parking garage nearby and drove up all 15 levels to the top, where there would be no cars around.

For some reason we didn't think to change in the bathroom while we were at In-N-Out, but we decided to take turns in the van. The guys went first, so the girls wouldn't be stuck outside in the cold waiting for us in their dresses. It was a frigid 30 degrees and the wind was gusting up to 30mph. It surely felt as though the temperature was in it's teens, which is exceptionally cold for Las Vegas. Bobby,

Cameron and I changed into our dress clothes, which we had somewhat coordinated ahead of time, but mostly worked with what we had. Surprisingly, we looked good. We looked really good. We were all in black and white. I owned a handful of vests and ties I had bought in the past for weddings I had participated in, and they were coming in handy. I was wearing my full black suit with a white button up shirt, a white vest along with a black tie. Cameron wore black dress pants and a white dress shirt, along with a black vest and black tie. Bobby wore a pair of black dress pants, A white dress shirt, black suspenders along with a black bow tie. While we all looked different, our outfits complemented each-other very well. It looked as though we put far more thought into it than we actually did.

We were all dressed and ready to go. We simultaneously exited the van in the most fashionable way possible to show the girls we were ready for showtime and it was their turn to get ready. They were shivering as they waited outside, bundled up in their winter jackets. Without acknowledging how awesome we looked, they gleefully jumped into the van and started it up so they could run the heater as they applied some makeup and changed into their dresses.

Meanwhile, us guys wandered around near the elevator far enough away from the van so we could keep an eye on it without seeing inside. We wanted to make sure nobody was going to casually come to where we parked and see them changing in the van.

Cameron, Bobby and I stood near the elevator where we could stay out of the cold wind. It was not only freezing cold, but it was also incredibly windy. This wasn't the Las Vegas I was familiar with. It was typically at least moderately warm. This weather was unbearably cold.

While we did our best to warm ourselves as much as possible, we waited patiently. We continued waiting. We waited still. We began wondering if the girls missed the memo that this wasn't going to be a real wedding. They were taking an exceptionally long time. I looked at my phone. It was almost midnight. I was hoping beyond hope that we would be able to find an Elvis impersonator somewhere. Anywhere. This was Las Vegas. They've got to be everywhere, right?

After what felt like eternity, the girls finally came out of the van. Cara was wearing a black mid-length dress. She had done an excellent job presenting herself as a bridesmaid. Larissa had a beautiful white mid-length dress and a clip with a veil attached that she had found at the mall the previous week. She had white high heels on to accent the attire. Her hair was done up and she looked incredibly beautiful. Her dress didn't look like a traditional wedding dress, but it looked more like the kind of dress a girl would buy on a whim if she was about to elope. Perfect! With the veil and the bouquet she was holding, this was looking not only legitimate, but we all made this look really good. If we were actually eloping, we would be doing it better than anybody else could dream of.

Cara had rented a high-end camera to use for the trip. She picked it out of her bag, only to realize the camera did not include a memory card, rendering the camera useless at this point. We were disappointed, but we didn't allow it to slow us down. We had our cell phones, and they would be able to get the pictures we needed. We figured we could get a memory card the next morning.

We made our way to the garage elevator. The girls were already shivering and I couldn't help but feel sorry for them. They were wearing their jackets, but their legs were completely exposed to the cold desert wind. We took the elevator to ground level and pioneered our way to Fremont street. We walked as fast as the girls were able to keep up with in their heels. After walking a few blocks, we found our way to the dead center of Fremont street. The "street" wasn't open to traffic. It was closed off as an open walkway for tourists to easily walk from one casino to the other.

As we stopped to look around hoping to find the best place for us to go find an Elvis, a group of people on a balcony across the street started cheering for us. "Whoooo! Congratulations!! They just got married!!" They yelled to us on the street below as loud as they could. There was actually a considerable amount of people cheering. It felt pretty good. We all glanced at each other and laughed. I threw my hand in the air and waved to them as though to say "Thank you." I allowed them think what they wanted. We were up to something far more elaborate than what they realized.

We walked up the street in search of an Elvis impersonator. Sure, it was very late at night, and there were not very many people out on the street, but I was convinced there was bound to be one somewhere nearby. Realistically, it was after midnight and tourists were either in bars or already at their hotel sleeping. Logically thinking, this wouldn't be an ideal time for an Elvis to be standing outside trying to get tourists to tip them money for a photo. Maybe we would have better luck if we went into the different casinos. This is Vegas. Elvis is somewhere. The girl's feet were starting to hurt from walking in their heels, and of course they were cold and starting to feel miserable. The girls decided to hang out at the Golden Nugget Casino while we walked around inside every different casino hoping to find our guy. We walked from one end of the street to the other, and back again, looking through every place we could find in hopes of having some luck.

Meanwhile, back at the Golden Nugget, the girls were having luck of their own, where they took a dollar and turned it into five pennies. That was the extent of their gambling, fortunately, but at least they were having fun on their own.

Bobby knew this was a lost cause. It was after 1:00 in the morning and we were just wasting our time. He told me we would need to just take photos without Elvis, but that wasn't good enough for me. We *needed* Elvis.

"He's out there. Somewhere. This is Las Vegas! Elvis's are everywhere!" I told him. I was determined to find one.

After another 20 minutes of trying to find one, Bobby approached me again. "Tom. It's late. It's cold. The girls are tired. We need to just get these photos done and head to LA."

"Yeah." I conceded. I had to admit this was a lost cause. The photos just wouldn't quite be everything I pictured, but we would still be able to accomplish what I intended. "Let's go get the girls."

Bobby, Cameron, and I went to find the girls. We could tell they were wearing out, but still seemed to be in good spirits. "We can't find an Elvis, and it doesn't look like we're going to," I told them.

Cameron chimed in. "All the Elvis's are sleeping."

"Let's just go get some photos done in a nice area, put them online and we'll head to LA in time for us to eat breakfast." I decided.

While the girls waited, Bobby, Cameron, and I went in search of an ideal location to take photos. Within ten minutes we were able to find a lobby with beautiful marble floor, an incredible crystal chandelier, and enormous black pillars.

Once the girls joined us, we began taking photos. We posed for several photos, doing our best to resemble what any person would expect to see after a wedding. I had a few photos taken with the guys celebrating this enormous achievement with our hands on each other's shoulders, another with them holding me upside down, just being silly. We did a traditional bouquet toss, which was quite comical since Cara was the only girl there to catch it. Then we asked the desk receptionist get group photos of us all together.

After roughly a half hour of us having fun taking these random photos, it was time to head to LA. It was roughly 2:30 AM and we wanted to get there at a somewhat decent time in the morning. Cameron, Bobby and I went to get the van while the girls waited in the lobby. We figured we may as well pick them up rather than having them walk all the way back to the van in the cold night air.

After we climbed into the van and spiraled down all 15 stories of the garage, we picked up Larissa and Cara at the casino and headed for the interstate. We were on the way to California and on track to accomplish our next major feat.

We were all very tired, as Bobby drove the van southwest on I-15 toward Los Angeles. It was 3AM, which meant it felt like 6AM for us, since we had arrived from the east coast. If there was anything I didn't factor into the initial 24 hours of the trip, it was sleep. (Something I don't take into serious consideration when I plan such adventures). This time, there just wasn't time for it. We didn't want to shell out too much money for hotels, either. The only opportunity for anyone to sleep was in the van as we were on the way to Los Angeles.

Not long after we started driving, we had a small celebration as we passed a sign welcoming us to California. I congratulated Bobby and Cara on their first time there.

Cara and Larissa napped the best they could as we made our way towards Los Angeles. Cameron and I stayed awake so we could enjoy the scenery as the sun came up, but also give Bobby some company as he drove. As the sun came up it revealed snow capped mountains in the nearby horizon and more incredible scenery that continued to blow Bobby's mind. We were all in California, highly anticipating our travels to come, for various reasons. I was especially looking forward to the next evening, when I would be asking Larissa the biggest question of our lives.

CHAPTER 10
The Proposal

By the time we cruised into LA on the 210 at 7AM, we were all wide awake and ready for the day. Except for Larissa. In addition to of her lack of sleep, she was still feeling sick. The combination of walking around in freezing temperatures and long strenuous hours of being awake were not helping her fight it.

We had plans to meet with Bobby and Larissa's birth father later in the morning at a Starbucks in Burbank. He lived in Santa Clarita working as a machinist for an airplane parts manufacturer. It had been years since he had seen his children.

Before our rendezvous, we needed to run to Target so Cara could pick up a memory card for the nice camera she rented. While we were there, we changed out of our fake elopement attire and prepared for another adventurous day.

After getting the memory card and other essentials, we decided to grab breakfast at Ihop. Ever since we posted our fake elopement pictures to Facebook and Instagram, we had all been receiving numerous text messages and voicemails from our friends and family who were hopelessly confused. We sat at the table joking about all the reactions we were getting. Numerous texts of people asking if what they had seen was for real, giving us a congratulations, while some of our friends and family were simply confused and wanted to know what was happening. The pictures we posted on Instagram and Facebook were receiving all the same reactions. My friends and family were baffled. Some of them fully believed we were married now. Others weren't sure what to think. The true question in their mind was if Larissa and I were crazy enough to elope, or if we were so crazy we would be willing to fly out to Las Vegas just so we could pretend to.

Best of all was multiple voicemails from Larissa's youngest sister, Tesla. She left several voicemails on everyone's phone except for me and Cameron, trying to understand what was going on and why she wasn't told about it. With the horrible people we are, we played them on speaker phone for us all to hear and laugh over. Every voicemail she left displayed a different reaction. Her first voicemail sounded like she was whining while breaking out in tears. "Larissa, can you please tell me what's going on? We're all worried and we just need to hear from you. Please call me. I love you." In her next voicemail she was very angry. "You're awful! I hate you! I thought we were best friends! You promised I would be in your wedding someday! We're sisters!! How could you do this to me?! I hate you!" I felt somewhat horrible at this point. Meanwhile, Bobby was across the table exploding in laughter, which made me feel somewhat less horrible of a person. He started relentlessly impersonating her voicemail. Seeing how he reacted made me feel at least like a half decent human being.

Meanwhile the phone rang again. Tesla was making another attempt to reach us. Naturally, we ignored it. In a few minutes we had another joyous voicemail to listen to. This one she was sympathetic as she regretted saying the hateful words that she had said earlier. "I don't hate you, Larissa. I'm sorry I said that. I didn't mean it. I'm really sorry. We just really, really want to know what's going on. Please, please, please call us. We're all really worried. You guys just really need to call us."

Bobby laughed loudly and relentlessly started imitating Tesla's new voicemail. I had been feeling like a horrible person with the voicemails and text messages that had been coming in, but seeing Bobby's carefree reaction helped me to shake off any of the guilt I was feeling and enjoy myself. All this confusion would soon end when I had the opportunity to share with everyone the news of the proposal. I knew I needed to ignore the negativity we were receiving at the moment. It would only be temporary.

After finishing up our breakfast and spending more time reading the comments posted on the pictures we posted onto social media, we paid for our bill and went across the street to Starbucks. Larissa and Bobby's birth father, Allan arrived a few minutes after we did. Allan was clearly a Harley Davidson enthusiast. He wore blue jeans, a jean jacket, over top his black Hell's Angel's tee shirt. He wore a black leather vest with various motorcycle-related patches all over it. He had an earring in each ear, a beard that was going gray, and he wore a black hat to cover his balding head.

After Larissa introduced us to each-other we enjoyed our time sitting and visiting. As we talked, it was very interesting being able to study Allan and see what features, and person-ality quirks Larissa had inherited from him. His jokes were somewhat vulgar and unfiltered. I could tell he was overjoyed with this opportunity to visit with Larissa and Bobby again. I could tell he regretted the decisions he had made in the past, but he was clearly a different man. He was fully determined to get things right in his life. More than anything, he wanted to mend the broken relationships he had with his children.

With only one full day to enjoy in Los Angeles, I wanted to make the best of it and take everyone to the best spots. First we would go to City Walk at Universal Studios to see all the shops, the indoor skydiving, and all the tourist attrac-tions. We would then go to Hollywood Boulevard to observe the Walk of Fame, then maybe drive around until we found a close spot to the Hollywood sign so we could take pictures with it. I just needed to time everything right so we could go to the hike for the sunset, so I could propose in the perfect moment. Timing was everything.

At this point, I wasn't sure if Larissa had caught onto my ultimate plan for this trip. As Bobby had told me in a con-versation a few days prior, "If she doesn't know by now that she's getting proposed to on this trip, she's about as dumb as a brick."

I had done my best to otherwise not lead her on to the fact that I was ready to propose. I had stopped talking about marriage altogether and left her in somewhat of a limbo. She was fully convinced I wanted to visit her family on 10 separate occasions, which gave us at least seven more trips to make.

Just in case she had any bit of an inkling that I was going to propose, I wanted to make sure the moment would at least catch her off guard. I needed the hike to seem as though it was a spontaneous idea. To prepare for this, I gave my friend Allyson a task to help set us up for the hike. The plan was that we would be meeting with her around 4:00 and she would take us on a hike to go see a waterfall. At 3:30 she would call me and make up some excuse as to why she wasn't able to join us. After I received that call I would ask the others what they wanted to do, so whatever we did, it wouldn't seem as though it was my idea. It was then to be Cara's job to ask if there was a hike we could take to overlook the city so she could try out the new lenses she had for her camera. Cameron and Bobby would be aware of this plan and automatically agree that doing this hike would be a good idea. I would then "know of a place" and take us to the trail that would lead us to the city overlook, where I would propose.

After finishing our drinks and spending quality time in conversation, it was time for us to set out for City Walk. We invited Bobby and Larissa's birth father, Allan, to come along with us. I figured it would surely mean a lot to him to be able to spend more time with his kids. He was very enthusiastic about the invitation and was more than happy to join us. Surprisingly in the time he had been living in California, he hadn't gone to any of the popular touristy places around LA. He really didn't come across as the kind of person to have any desire to see them anyway.

When we arrived at the Jurassic Parking outside Universal Studios, we walked out to the retail districts of City Walk. We were mesmerized by all the fabulous restaurants, shops, and beautiful architecture. We stopped to watch somebody do the indoor skydiving in the clear vertical wind tunnel. It was something we all wished we could do but we didn't have the budget for it. We continued exploring the different souvenir shops. This was all familiar to Larissa as we were there on our first date and I had bought her a purple "Hollywood" hoodie.

After an hour of admiring the different attractions, we were feeling satisfied with what we had seen in City Walk. We decided it was time to move on to our next stop. This was our only day in Los Angeles, so I wanted to make sure Bobby and Cara both had the chance to see as much as possible, since it was their first time in California.

The next item on our list was the Hollywood Walk of Fame. We went back to our vehicles and drove towards Hollywood Blvd. Once we parked in the Hollywood and Highland garage, we walked out to the Walk of Fame. Even though I had been there several times before, the hand prints in the cement from celebrities of our generation and the generations before us always stood out as a reminder of the historical significance of where we were. Meanwhile, Cara wandered around snapping photos of us, the handprints of different celebrities, and anything else that caught her attention.

It was almost lunch time, and since we were so low on sleep, we needed to eat some food to fuel ourselves through the rest of the day. We found a mexican fast food restaurant nearby and headed there to eat. As we walked to the restaurant we observed the various stars in the sidewalk featuring a different name of a celebrity on each of them. After our brief walk, we stepped into the restaurant. Allan was kind enough to pay for all of our meals, and as we ate our tacos and burritos, we allowed ourselves to take the time to enjoy our meal and visit. It was enjoyable learning more about Allan. I could tell this visit he was having with Larissa and Bobby was one of the best things to happen to him in a long time.

After we finished visiting over our meal, we headed back to the Hollywood and Highland Shopping area. This area has a wide open spot with fountains, decorated architecture celebrating the glamorous history, as well as an observation point to see the Hollywood Sign. We still had a couple hours to kill before the proposal and there was limited options of what we could do within the time frame. We decided to wander around in the Hollywood Hills in search of a good photo location so we could get close-up photos with the Hollywood Sign.

With Allan following closely behind us, we drove around using Google Earth to help us find the right location for photos. As we were driving, we shared our thoughts about how people were reacting to the fake elopement. I still felt somewhat guilty about doing it, since I was getting all these texts and voicemails. My heart would throb every time my phone would buzz with a new voicemail or text. By now Larissa didn't even care anymore. She felt as though people were overreacting and making a much bigger deal about it than it needed to be.

I asked Bobby to share how he felt. "Well." he began "A prank is a prank is a prank. I think this is all in good fun, and everybody is just freaking out about it." Well said, I guess. At least Bobby's guilt free approach put me somewhat at ease. I was sure people's concerns would be put to rest when they found out it wasn't for real. After all, when Larissa and I would turn out to be engaged and not married, people wouldn't have anything to be upset about. I just needed to keep that in mind as I pushed through these last few hours. The final pieces of the plan I had been assembling over the last seven months were about to come together.

After a half hour of driving, guessing, and trying different areas, we finally arrived at the perfect location that provided a close up view of the Hollywood sign. There were already a few people there, as it seemed to be the ideal location. On the side of the street toward the sign, there was a steep bank with houses below. Standing at the edge of the embankment directly across from us was the famous Hollywood Sign.

On the other side of the street were several small homes. For being in an expensive area such as "The Hollywood Hills," they certainly weren't much to look at. The houses were obviously sitting there for several decades and the ground they'd been built on was clearly worth far more than the houses themselves. The owners must have been used to people crowding the street in front of their home.

When we stepped out of the van, Cara began snapping photos as we posed at the edge of the road with the Hollywood Sign directly behind us. It's only when you start getting this close to the sign that you realize just how large the individual letters are.

After we enjoyed a decent amount of time having fun getting our photos taken, I looked at my phone. It was still vibrating from time to time with texts, calls, and notifications of my friends and family trying to figure out what was going on. I swiped a few more new notifications aside to see the time. We were barely past 3:00. I had burned the perfect amount of time for us to start heading back to Burbank and prepare for our hike. We all bid farewell to Allan as we climbed back into our rental van.

We headed back to Burbank Town Center Mall so we could freshen up before our "hike with Allyson". We parked and headed to the restrooms. I pulled out the ring for Bobby and Cameron to observe. My heart was beginning to throb at the thought of proposing. "You got this, man." Bobby said, doing his best to put me at ease. I nodded. I knew I had to just do this and shake off any nervous feelings. Bobby gave me a strong pat on the back and a respectful nod before we headed back out the door. Larissa and Cara stepped out of their restroom a few minutes later and we headed back to the van.

As soon as we were out of the parking garage and on the way to Allyson's house, my phone started vibrating with a call from Allyson. "Hey Allyson, what's up?" I answered with enthusiasm. "Hey Tom, I'm really sorry, but I'm not going to be able to do the hike today. My dog threw up all over the carpet, and it's going to take me a lot of time to clean it up. I'm really sorry."

"Oh wow, that totally sucks. I'm so sorry to hear that." I responded doing the best I could to sound natural. I was always a horrible actor and I knew it. "We can find something else to do and kill some time. Do you think you might still be able to meet up with us later?"

"Yeah, I should be able to. This will just take some time to clean up." she said doing her best to sound authentic. She sounded more genuine than I did.

"It's all good" I assured her. "We can find something to do in the meantime," I said as I hung up the phone. I relayed the message to everyone in the van. "Soooo Allyson's dog threw up all over their carpet and she needs some time to get it cleaned up. We need to get something else figured out." I explained to everyone.

"That's the dumbest thing I've ever heard!" Larissa exclaimed. Apparently not only am I a horrible actor, but I apparently suck at writing scripts.

"Well, that's what she told me." I stated assertively, while sticking to the original story. I figured it was reasonable to allow Larissa assume Allyson was a horrible person for at least a few hours until she understood everything. "Do any of you have ideas on what you'd like to do to kill some time?" I casually asked the group as I continued my act.

Cara was quick to speak up as she recognized her cue "Are there any good places we could hike to where we would overlook the city? I'd love to capture some photos of the city lights with these lenses I brought with me."

Larissa immediately gave her a death stare. She was feeling completely exhausted, and was still feeling very sick. The last thing she wanted to do was go on a hike.

"Yeah, I think I know of a hike that would be perfect for that." I replied. "Do you guys think that would be a good idea?"

Bobby and Cameron went right along with what I told them they were to do and agreed that taking a hike to overlook the city was the perfect idea.

Meanwhile, Larissa was pleading not to do a hike because of how awful she had been feeling. Unfortunately/fortunately for her, she was in the minority. Four out of five of us had decided that we would all be going on a hike, so her rejection to the idea was fruitless.

"Sounds good. I know of a really good spot. It's not too bad of a hike, and it has stunning views. It'll be perfect!" I said as I could see the disappointment in Larissa's eyes. It truly was unfortunate she was feeling so awful, but she had no idea this hike was about to be one of the highlights of her life. She had been hoping for a long time that I would propose, and if she knew that was the plan, she would have been advocating for the hike more than anybody else, no matter how sick she felt. She would reach the top with a fresh layer of makeup before anybody else would have the chance to get started.

I drove us up into the hillside of Burbank and headed towards the city limits of Glendale where Brand Library Park was located. Since we were in the month of December, the sun would be setting relatively early. We needed to make sure we could get to the lookout before that happened.

Larissa began to try and talk her way out of hiking with us since she had been feeling so sick and exhausted. As we approached the climax of my elaborate plan, the only thing that could possibly go wrong at this point would be if Larissa refused to go on the hike. Fortunately Cara and Bobby knew how to use their psychological warfare to sway her into climbing out of the van to join us. She grumbled as she stepped out of the mini-van. I couldn't help but be entertained by her lack of will power at this point. Not because I enjoy watching her suffer, but because of how clueless she was as to what was about to happen.

We grabbed a few extra bottles of water and began making our way up the hill. I carried the ring in it's case in my pocket, doing my best to be sure it wasn't noticeable. As we made our way up the mountain I looked in the far distance of where we were heading. Somehow the only thing I ever remembered about the hike was the view at the end, and not how grueling of a trek it was to get there. I always pictured it as a hike that was relatively easy, but I was always far off on my expectations. I was having a difficult time catching my breath as we paced our way to our destination. Even though I was an avid rock climber and snowboarder among other things with a decent muscular tone, cardio was never a strength. Nor was it something I ever cared to exercise. I hated running, and my lack of cardiovascular exercise was becoming very evident as I was having a difficult time catching my breath as we ascended this mountain.

I began feeling nervous about the proposal. I didn't have any doubt that she would say "yes", but even so, the weight of this loaded question was bearing down on me. This was the only time I would ever be asking this question. She was the only one I wanted to spend the rest of my life with. This was a big deal. I pressed on as the weight of the anticipation continued to build.

"Guys, I really don't think I want to do this." Larissa exclaimed as we had progressed up the mountain quite a ways, and she was just as far out of breath as I was. I could see the exhaustion in her face. Feeling sick, along with a lack of sleep, was taking a heavy toll.

Bobby chimed in with a chant to push her to the top. "No sacrifice, no victory!!" he exclaimed as Larissa was oblivious to the real meaning behind his statements. He laughed at her obvious suffering and obliviousness to what was going on. Fortunately, he had a strong element of sibling rivalry he and Larissa had grown up with. He egged her on to suck it up and reach the top. Surely Larissa knew if she couldn't complete this hike, she would be hearing about it from him for a long time.

Cara had been joyfully snapping photos as we all progressed up the mountain. As Larissa's motivation continued to dwindle, Cara held back to give her a few words of encouragement. Things at this point would obviously fall apart if Larissa decided not to come to the lookout point with us.

We eventually came to a leveled off area. There were four cement pillars that stood as supports to a fire tower that had burned away decades earlier. Each of the pillars were about four feet tall, providing a convenient place to rest and lean on. Larissa hopped up to sit on one of the pillars as she felt a tremendous amount of relief. Her legs were burned out, and she was feeling even more sick and exhausted. "Okay." She said as she was panting, completely out of breath. "We made it." She tried to fake a smile, but we could all see right through it.

"Oh, we're not there yet." I told her as I pointed to an outcropping further up the mountain. "That's where we're headed."

Her eyes widened further than I had ever seen. She lifted her arm in a slow and droopy motion and pointed to the outcropping. "All the way up there?" She asked feeling completely disheartened. The last time I saw her this disappointed was when I had her convinced I wouldn't be proposing to her anytime soon.

"No way." She stated affirmatively. "There's no way I'm walking all the way up there. I'm sick. I'm tired. My phone won't stop ringing. Everybody hates us. I'm going to wait here for you guys to go up to the top, get your pictures and come back down. I'll be waiting right here for you."

With all the challenges I had faced and overcome in the process of assembling this plan to propose to Larissa, I did not expect this to be the crux of this grand scheme. I wasn't even sure what I would do if Larissa did not reach the top. Our current view was not nearly as beautiful of a view and was very undeserving of hosting such a life changing event.

"Come on, hun." I insisted. "I promise it'll be worth it. The view is really good, I promise. And after we get back down you can rest up feeling accomplished." I gently grabbed her hand and guided her off the cement pillar. "Come on, you can do this. I believe in you. There's benches up there and we can rest up for as long as you need. I promise you, the hike will be worth it." I told her as we continued with the final stretch of our surprisingly intense hike.

Bobby chimed in again doing his best to flex his muscle of sibling rivalry. "If you don't make it to the top, you're definitely going to miss out. But you can stay right here if you're too weak to make it to the top."

Larissa glared at Bobby as she shifted off of the cement pillar and reluctantly continued on the hike with us. As we began to progress up the mountain, I couldn't help but mess with the ring in it's case. I felt like I had to continually shift it into different pocket's when Larissa wasn't looking so I wouldn't have an obvious bulge, revealing the cargo I had with me.

I continued to take deep breaths to keep my nervousness from becoming apparent. As we walked up the mountain, I lingered behind with Bobby, as he made sure to keep Larissa motivated enough to prevent her from turning around. When Larissa wasn't looking I would step forward and do lunges, bringing my knee to the ground in an effort to prepare my body for what felt like would be the most awkward thing in the world. When am I ever down on one knee? This is somewhat of a weird concept, right? The process of getting down on one knee was feeling extremely foreign all of a sudden.

This was going be the only time in my life I would be getting on one knee with the intent of asking a serious, life-changing question. I had to keep reminding myself which knee I was supposed to go down on. It would be my left knee. Of course I had googled it about a month before, to be certain. The concept still felt weird to me, but I guess it's what I'm supposed to do. I wasn't about to screw it up just because it felt weird.

With enough motivation, Larissa completed the final ascent with the rest of us. As we reached the observation point, we sat on the bench to rest and catch our breath. Meanwhile, Bobby and Cameron strolled around taking in the views. Cara struck conversation with another photographer who had also come up to take photographs of the city lights.

The sun was beginning to set, allowing the city lights to shine brighter. The sunset wasn't anything glorious. It was a typical California sunset with a gradient of yellow and orange. Without variance in the weather or clouds in the sky, a spectacular sunset is hard to come by. I was figuring if it was an incredible sunset I would propose with it as the backdrop, but if not, I could wait just a little longer and propose with the lights of the city in the background.

Being December in California, it still cooled off quite a bit. The air was dry, but it was still right around 50 degrees. Even though we were in the sunny state of California, we still needed jackets to keep warm. I took my jacket off and laid it on the bench to prepare for what would be coming next.

I walked Larissa to the edge of the lookout to position ourselves for the proposal. As Larissa and I stood there, she asked about the different areas of the city we were overlooking.

I pointed out Burbank below us, Glendale to the left, North Hollywood and Van Nuys were straight out. In the distance to our left we could see the skyscrapers of Downtown Los Angeles. I pointed out the large hill across from us to her informing her the Hollywood sign was directly on the opposite side. The lights of the city went further than our eyes could see. Cars traveled down the interstates, making them look as if they were flowing rivers of light.

"It's cold. We should get going." Larissa said as she began to turn back to the bench where we were seated earlier.

"What's the craziest thing you've ever done?" I asked her casually as I gently grabbed her arm to keep her from stepping away.

"Fake eloped." She said without hesitation. "You keep one-upping yourself." She said with a laugh. "I don't understand."

"Mind if I dare you to do something crazier?" I asked with a grin I couldn't stop from spreading on my face.

"Don't you dare!" She exclaimed. "Stop! Walk away.. Walk away.." Larissa began nervously trying to turn away from me as I did my best to gently hold her in place for what was coming next. Apparently at this point she was convinced I was still all 'fun and games' and was convinced I was asking her to be my fake fiance so we could carry on with this cruel joke we played on our family and friends..

"I dare you to be my wife," I said as the grin on my face became a full-fledged smile. I was in the process of accomplishing possibly the greatest feat of my entire life. I subtly reached into my pocket to grab the black velvet ring box.

"You're kidding! Stop it!" She said in a curious, yet nervous panic as I pulled out the box and proceeded to get down on my left knee (which felt as weird as I expected it to).

"Holy crap! Stop! No! Please don't! Oh my gosh! Tom you're joking." Larissa was almost pleading with me at this point. The words she was speaking were immediately deflected by my bulletproof ego, as every crazy aspect of my plan had come together flawlessly up to this point. I confidently proceeded as I knew Larissa was having difficulty grasping the reality of the moment.

"Larissa Marie Godfrey-Sutton," I said proudly as I opened the case to display the dazzling engagement ring. "You're the love of my life, will you marry me?" I said with an enormous grin as I knew she did not see this coming. Even though at this point it was sounding like a flat out rejection, I was now on one knee holding out a ring with every bit of confidence I had when I purchased the flights for our first date.

As soon as I asked her the life-changing question she went silent. I remained patiently on one knee holding out a diamond engagement ring, as her frazzled and exhausted mind began to register what was happening in front of her.

Larissa was literally speechless, with absolutely no words she could come up with say as she cupped her hands over her face. Her eyes welled up in tears as she nodded yes, as she was at such a loss for words, it was all she could bring herself to do. I practically leapt from my position and embraced her as emotion of the moment ran through me.

"Oh my gosh." She could barely say as she was now sobbing uncontrollably, in addition to losing her voice from being so sick and exhausted. "This was not at all how I planned it." She said before taking another deep breath. In her head, she had her own idea on how the proposal was going to happen, and how she would react. I couldn't have caught her further off guard.

"How long have you planned this?" She asked through her continuing tears. Now she was curious how I brought this all together.

"When we planned the fake eloping." I stated as tears were beginning to run down my face as well.

"Holy crap, Tom…" She said in a sigh. "What?!!" All of a sudden she was hit with a realization. "That was.. That was two weeks after we started dating!"

"Oh I know.. I was like 'Eh, I've taken bigger risks.'" I said with a laugh as my voice continued with a slight tremble. "I told myself that if I was going to propose to you, I wanted to take you back out to LA to do this, and I would need to come with some kind of plan."

We looked at each-other and laughed in complete joy. She took a step back. "Here!" She said as she put her hand out towards me. "You can put it on my finger, and then you're going to put it back in the box. So it doesn't get ruined. Actually no, let's just put it on." Now her mind was racing at 100mph.

"Let's do this the right way." I said as I got back down on my knee to put it on. It fit her perfectly. "It even fits. As though it was made just for you."

"Oh my gosh." She said "Oh my gosh!" She said in a soft, squeally voice. "Thank you. I don't know what else to say." We embraced again. "Oh my gosh, I can't- I don't- I don't deserve you. This shouldn't be happening. I don't deserve you. I really don't." Larissa's brain was in hyperdrive, as she was saying anything that came to her mind as she was having a difficult time comprehending all that had just happened. Just when she had almost regained her composure, she leaned into my shoulder and began sobbing again in my arms.

Meanwhile, the photographer who had been at this location before us was no longer being subtle, as he was clearly snapping countless photos of us. At this point he was only 10 feet away, crouching for the best shot he could get of us. As the moment was beginning to calm down, I felt it was probably an ideal time to let her know this photographer wasn't a stranger that happened to be there at random.

"By the way." I said just as Larissa was beginning to take notice of the photographer who was now busy snapping away multiple photos of us "This is my friend, Robert Brett."

"Oh my gosh!!! No!!!" She exclaimed as she was completely taken aback by all that was brought together. "I can't believe you brought me all the way up here un-showered! I'm filthy!"

At this point Cara, Bobby, and Cameron had made their way back to us. We all laughed as Larissa was making multiple teary-eyed, startled comments.

"I'm so glad we fake eloped!" Larissa said.

"You know there was no way we could ever get away with that unless we came back engaged, right?" I joked. It was a relief to finally have all of this out in the open. I was getting so tired of keeping secrets. I had just spent almost 8 months refraining from sharing the biggest secret of my life with everyone, even my best friend.

"Here. Hold onto the ring. I'm afraid I'm going to lose it on the hike down." Larissa said as she attempted to hand the ring over.

"You don't want to wear it?" I asked her.

"I do, just not when we're hiking" She said.

"Hold onto it for now." I told her. "We're going to do a photoshoot."

"Not like this!!!" She panically exclaimed. None of us had showered in at least a day and a half. We had all sweated it out on the hike up the mountain, and of course when I proposed to Larissa, her tears and attempts to wipe away tears smeared two days worth of makeup around her eyes to the point she looked like a raccoon.

"It's alright" I assured her. "We need to get photos of us up here. I promise, his photos are phenomenal. This is going to be worth it, I promise. Cara is going to get more engagement photos of us as we go up along the coast the next couple days. We can be more prepared for photos then."

Larissa reluctantly went along with me so Robert could get some photos of us together. Since the sun had gone down completely it was starting to get noticeably colder and darker. Robert had several lenses, a tripod, as well as a large white umbrella shaped fabric to be used as the flash for the camera. All of his equipment was top notch. I had seen his incredible work where he would light up the foreground in the photo and still capture city lights, or even stars in the background. Being familiar with his previous work, I knew he would be able to get the exact photos I was hoping to get. His work was always as breath-taking as seeing things first-hand.

Larissa and I started off posing for a few different photos of us embracing, another photo of me on one knee, and some more of us holding each-other with the ring clearly visible. All of the photos were taken as a long exposure to capture the light of the city in the background, and during the long exposure, he would set off the bright flash, to make us clear in the foreground. Cara watched him work as she gathered techniques for her to apply with her photography.

After Larissa and I had a few dozen photos taken, we had Cameron, Cara, and Bobby come over to get a photo with us. As an accomplished team, we stood together arm-in-arm with big smiles on our faces reflecting the mission we had accomplished. Robert took a few more photos using the long exposure with flash, and we decided it was time to wrap things up. While everyone else helped Robert pack up his photography equipment, Larissa and I walked away from everyone so we could make a few phone calls.

My mom had been attempting to call throughout the day and texted me a handful of times to find out if we had gotten married, or what exactly was going on. Of course, her phone had been endlessly ringing from relatives asking her for information she was dying to find out for herself. I almost felt uneasy as I began to call her. Especially since I was certainly putting her through more stress than she had faced in years. I was at least feeling satisfaction in the fact that I could finally give her a response and deliver some exciting news that would help her sleep at night.

After only a couple of rings, she picked up the phone. "About time you got back to me." She started off with a stern voice. "What exactly is going on?" She asked. I could tell she was tired.

"Well" I started off "Larissa and I aren't married. But we are engaged!" I said with some enthusiasm, but not too much, since I wanted to match her tone to at least some extent. She was sounding exhausted, and certainly bothered by what was going on. The only sense of relief I was feeling at this point was the fact that Larissa and I hadn't actually eloped. This was the kind of disappointment I knew I would face, but worse.

"I'm glad to hear you're engaged. But why did you have to run off without telling anyone and pretend you got married?! I've been getting calls and texts from relatives all day of people trying to find out what was going on, and I had to tell them I didn't know any more than they did!" She sounded as though she was both tired and stressed out.

"Well," I began to explain "I wanted to propose to Larissa here in California, and so I talked her into fake eloping so she wouldn't be expecting it."

It was still difficult for her to feel happy for me at this point after the stressful day she had but she definitely put forth her best effort. "Well, I'm glad to hear you're engaged. Tell Larissa congratulations for me. It's good to know what is going on."

"Thanks mom." I said. "Would you be able to put Dad on the phone?"

"Him and Sam are hunting at Tom McNutt's." she told me. "You'll have to call them separately." So that meant they were in the western part of Pennsylvania nowhere near my mom. I quickly wrapped up the conversation as I saw everybody was ready to head back down to the parking. Before we started helping them, I informed Larissa what was coming next. We would be heading to Bean Town in Sierra Madre to meet up with all of our local friends to celebrate the engagement. There was no better place to get together than the coffee shop we spent some of our time at on our first date. Everybody else already knew the plan. We grabbed our jackets, picked up some bags of the camera equipment, and started making our way down the hill.

As we helped Robert carry his equipment, we used our cell phones to light up the path ahead of us the best we could.

Several parts of it were very steep and tricky. The last thing we needed was to slip and fall while carrying his delicate equipment.

After finishing a gruelling hike down the mountain and feeling like our calves were ready to burst, we climbed back into the van and started making our way to Sierra Madre. As we drove, we made a few select phone calls to inform our families of our great news. Of course Larissa's family was left in the dark as well, so this would be a happy update for them. It was nearly 10:00 on the east coast, which was practically the middle of the night for the Sutton household. Regardless, this was news they needed to hear. We put it on speaker for all of us to listen in. Mrs. Sutton happened to still be awake. She had been staying up late after a stressful day waiting to hear some news of some kind.

"Hello?" She answered after a few rings.

"Hey Mom." Larissa began "Tom and I just wanted to share some news with you."

"That would be wonderful. The entire family is very interested to know what is going on." She said in a curious tone.

"Well, just so you know, we're not married," Larissa said before she paused for dramatic effect. "but we are engaged." Mrs. Sutton was overjoyed at the news. She explained how much commotion there had been throughout the family and admitted she was personally very concerned, but she was quite relieved to hear she didn't miss out on a wedding, and that a wedding was soon to come in the future.

"Is Dad still awake?" Larissa asked.

"He's not, but I could get him if you want." Mrs. Sutton said.

"Yeah, go ahead and put him on. I'm sure he wouldn't mind waking up to hear this news."

After about a minute Mr. Sutton got on the phone. "Hello?" he answered sleepily.

"Hey dad, this is Larissa. I just wanted to let you know that Tom and I are not married, but we are engaged." She said getting right to the point.

"Engaged? Really?!" He said with an excited tone in his voice. "The family has been really confused today. They thought you had gotten married."

"We did do a fake elopement." Larissa said "But that wasn't for real. Tom had talked me into it so I would come out here where he wanted to propose to me without me expecting it."

"Well I did think it was strange that he would ask me for my blessing and then run off and elope with you. That wasn't making any sense to me. None of us could believe Bobby would stand by and allow something like that to happen, either." Mr. Sutton explained.

At this point I whispered to everyone silently enough so I wouldn't be heard over the phone "I totally told him not to believe anything he heard until he heard it directly from us."

Larissa kindly repeated what I said to Mr. Sutton. He didn't recall me saying that, but admitted that he must have forgotten or not heard me among the washer running in the milkhouse. By the end of their conversation, Mr. Sutton was overjoyed at the fact that we were engaged.

After Larissa wrapped up her conversation with her dad, she asked him if Mary was available.

"She's asleep right now, but would you like me to get her anyway?" He asked.

"Yeah, I think she would like to hear about what is going on." Larissa said.

When Mary answered, she sounded not only tired, but as though every bit of enthusiasm had been drained out of her. She also questioned our need to fake elope, and when we briefly told her the story she said "Well, whatever. I'm happy for you guys. Congratulations." she said somewhat begrudgingly as she sounded half asleep with only a little bit of forced enthusiasm.

As we drove, we were getting close to Sierra Madre. I decided I should call my dad and deliver the news. I took a deep breath and dialed his number, as I had a distinct feeling that this conversation wasn't going to go as well as I had always imagined it would, especially after the tone of his voice in the message I received after the plane landed in Las Vegas. His phone rang and eventually went to voicemail. I tried again, and it went to voicemail again. My dad has never had voicemail set up, so I couldn't leave a message even if I wanted to. I called my brother Sam, since he was with him.

Sam answered, and I asked if he could put dad on the phone. "He's not ready to talk to you yet."

Ouch. I wasn't quite expecting that. "Well, could you tell him that Larissa and I are not married, and that we are engaged?" I asked him while informing him the news of what was really going on.

Sam told me he would tell him for me, but immediately drilled me about leaving the farm without calling off work, as well as getting the whole family up in arms about what I was doing. He really put a lot of emphasis on the time I was taking off, and had I set it up to be back Monday morning, it wouldn't have been as big of deal.

His aggressive approach caught me somewhat off-guard. I was expecting somewhat of a warmer response than that. In my head I had figured they would overlook the fact that I was leaving work unannounced since it was for such a good cause, and since we were family. Not to mention there's not a lot happening on a farm in December. A typical start to my day involved my dad scratching his head wondering what work he would have me do.

I wrapped up my conversation with Sam in an "Oh well" attitude, since there really wasn't much more I could do or say. I wasn't about to jump the next plane home just to make him and the rest of my family happy. I didn't want to allow such a conversation to bring me down and keep me from celebrating one of the most defining moments of my life.

We pulled into Sierra Madre as I wrapped up the conversation. We parked right across the street from Bean Town. The streets were lined with lamp posts and there were very few cars out. It was pleasant to be back in the town that feels so much like home.

As we stepped out of the van and walked across the street, I pushed all the guilt ridden feelings I had from the phone call behind me. Larissa and I were engaged and it was time to celebrate the occasion.

When we reached the other side of the street, we opened the door to Bean Town and all five of us walked in like rock stars as our friends cheered for us upon our entry. I had talked to all of my friends in LA about this after-party and a handful of them were able to be there to celebrate. We were immediately greeted by my old roommate, Joe and his wife. Natalie and Allyson waved to us from the back and quickly ran up to give us both a hug and congratulations. To the right we saw Steve Hardy, the artist we met at Bean Town on our first date. I had Joe invite him to join us for this event. When I saw him we went over to greet him. He told us how he could see the joy in our eyes and we had a bright future of love and adventure together.

After our conversation we moved on to greet Joe and his wife, whom I had yet to meet. Joe was the first person to ever mention the town of Sierra Madre to me when we had initially been roommates after I moved to California. He talked about this coffee shop "Bean Town" which I went on to discover later in my time living out there. Joe was a larger guy, much older than me. He was bald, and loved to play harmonica in his band. Robert Brett and his girlfriend were nearby to offer another round of congratulations.

We then had a chance to catch up with Allyson and Natalie. They were so excited for us. They immediately asked to see the ring I gave Larissa, as she was beyond excited to show it off to them. With our short time in LA, it was great to have a small handful of my friends together to visit with. While Larissa and I walked around chatting with friends, Cameron, Bobby, and Cara ordered some coffee and then took some time to mingle with some of our friends. Cara spent a lot of time with Bobby Brett to hear more about his experience with photography. Cameron was able to reconnect with Allyson and Natalie, since he had gotten to know them pretty well when he went on the road trip with me the year before.

Bobby hung with Cameron and the girls, and told stories of our experience so far on the trip. He always had a way of telling stories that had everyone laughing. It certainly helped relieve stress having Bobby along with us. Especially since he loves practical jokes and his enthusiasm toward the whole engagement mission helped me feel at ease, among the back-lash I was already facing from my family.

We spent another hour visiting with friends, swapping stories and celebrating the engagement. At this point it was getting late, and most of us hadn't managed to get any sleep since the night before we left, which was putting us right about at 40hrs without sleep. We were all exhausted. We said our goodbyes to all the friends who came to celebrate with us and I handed the keys over to Bobby as all of us headed to the van. As exhausted as I was feeling, I didn't feel like I could do the drive to Santa Monica. I set up the GPS for him and fell asleep in my seat before we even got to the freeway. We had about a half hour drive until we would get to the hotel I had reserved.

As Bobby drove, I felt myself go in and out of conscious-ness. Larissa and Cara were passed out in the center row, and Cameron just smiled, looking out the window while sitting quietly in the back. I'm not saying that because I saw him, but I know from experience, that's just what he does: sits qui-etly with a smile on his face. It's extremely rare for him to fall asleep in a moving vehicle.

When we arrived at the hotel in Santa Monica, I was ready to present one last surprise: An oceanview room for the girls. I brought my paperwork to the front desk to check in, as everybody else grabbed their luggage. I gave the girls their room key and I held onto the key for the room Bobby, Cameron, and I would be staying in.

Cameron, Bobby, and I helped Larissa and Cara with their bags and escorted them to their room. They couldn't even tell it was an ocean view because of how dark it was outside. Even if it was broad daylight I'm sure they would have barely noticed due to how exhausted they were. I said goodnight to my fiance and led the way to the other room.

There were three of us guys. I paid for the room. I definitely wasn't going to be sleeping on the floor. Bobby declared seniority over Cameron and snagged the other bed. Cameron didn't complain a single bit, as he always tends to be impressively selfless. He rolled out the sleeping bag, crawled in and went to sleep resting his head on a pillow I gave him from my bed.

I couldn't believe how exhausted we were. I couldn't believe the perfect execution of the engagement. I prayed to God thanking him for enabling all these amazing things to come together. There was no way I could have done this on my own.

We shut off the lights and effortlessly fell asleep. We had more traveling ahead of us, as we would be driving up the coast of California over the next couple days. We all wanted to make sure we could be as rested as possible.

CHAPTER 11
The Golden Coast

We awoke at 8:30 the next morning, even though I had planned for us to be out by 7:00 to begin our trek up the coast and get as much out of it as possible. Of course when I plan a trip, there's no such thing in my mind as being so terribly exhausted that you need to catch up on sleep. So I allowed us all to sleep longer and make sure we were well rested. And when I say "allowed us all to sleep longer", what I really mean is "Didn't bother to push my agenda because everybody would say I was out of my mind, ignore my plan, and sleep in anyway." Not to mention, I was extremely tired as well. I figured since this was also somewhat of a vacation, I needed to slow down and enjoy it. I didn't want to get in the way of anybody else enjoying themselves, either.

When I texted the girls to make sure they were ready to start their day, they were barely awake. Cara was actively packing her belongings while encouraging Larissa, who was still feeling sick and exhausted, to wake up and get her day going. After they were packed up and ready to go, they invited us into their room so we could see their oceanview. Straight ahead, we could clearly see the ocean, with palm trees in the foreground. Looking to the left was the Santa Monica Pier, and below us was Route 1: The infamous Pacific Coastal Highway we would be taking all the way to San Francisco. In the busy traffic below was a bright red Ferrari, standing among the other cars boldly making itself known. Bobby, Cameron and I gawked at it for a few brief seconds before it drove away.

We helped the girls carry their luggage down to the van and checked out of the hotel. Before we set off on the next extension of our journey, we headed out on foot in search of breakfast. We found a hipstery place to eat and sat down for our meal. There were several overpriced organic items to choose from, naturally with small portions. We each ordered our meals and enjoyed conversation with one another. We discussed everything that had transpired over the last couple days, as well as what our plans would be for the trip up the coast. When our small portions of food came out well decorated on the oddly shaped plates, Bobby blessed the food and we began eating our meals.

After enjoying breakfast, the girls wanted to go shopping since Larissa needed new clothes to wear for engagement photos. In the meantime, Cameron, Bobby and I wandered around the numerous shops in Downtown Santa Monica. As much as I wanted to hit the road and get started with our journey up the coast, I kept reminding myself to relax and avoid putting any stress on our time there. After we killed more time than I felt was necessary, we decided to check up on the girls, only to find them trying on clothes, barely making any progress. After they had finally picked out what they needed, we all headed back to the van. We wanted to get going, but since we weren't far from the pier, we decided to make one last stop before heading out.

Being December and an early Monday morning, this typically lively tourist attraction remained mostly vacant. We walked past the roller coaster and the Ferris Wheel, which makes the landmark so recognizable.

Larissa and I posed for photos at the end of the pier as Cara took some photos of us. Meanwhile Cameron and Bobby wandered around taking photos of their own while observing the ocean below.

After spending much of our time exploring and observing we were satisfied with the photos we had, and we were due to begin our journey up the coast. Our goal was to make it up to San Luis Obispo to visit my friend Michelle late in the evening, then find a place to camp somewhere on the beach.

Point Dume was only fifteen minutes up the road, and we figured that would be a great location to have some of our engagement photos taken. We had planned on getting photos done at several places as we progressed up the coast, and this would be our first stop.

We decided to check out the southern side of Point Dume, which I had never before seen. (Previously, I would always park at the beach and approach it from the North). We parked at the trailhead and walked down a short pathway until we found a long set of stairs leading to the beach below.

After all of us made it down the stairs and stepped onto the beach, Larissa and I headed to some rocks as Cara followed with her camera. Cara's photographer side came out as she began professionally instructing us on how to sit, how to look at each-other, and how we should pose for these engagement photos. She snapped away as we followed her instructions.

Meanwhile, Bobby and Cameron were carrying on, having fun of their own as they explored along the beach's giant boulders and magnificent cliffs. Cara continued encapturing photos of me and Larissa in various locations and poses. After we felt satisfied with our photoshoot, we headed back up the long stairs to level ground. Larissa found a small cactus and placed her ring on it's needles for Cara to get photos of it. Meanwhile, Bobby walked over to the cliffside and sat on the end of a drainage pipe that extended 8 feet beyond the edge of the cliff exposing him to a potential 60ft. drop. Even though I enjoyed taking risks of my own, I couldn't help but express concern for how many ways this could possibly go wrong. If the pipe gave way, it would certainly put a downer on the trip. He straddled the pipe with his arms in the air facing the pacific ocean as a temptation to fate.

I looked again at my phone to see what time it was. It was already early into the afternoon. We weren't nearly as far north as I had hoped to be, but I reminded myself yet again to relax and enjoy every moment. I knew I needed to enjoy where we were, making the best of every moment, and not rush things for the sake of seeing more. I looked closer again at our route, only to realize the Pacific Coastal Highway we were traveling on began to head inland half an hour north of Santa Barbara. We could enjoy the sunset there without missing too many sights on the coast. Michelle conveniently lived in part of that stretch, and after our visit with her in the evening, we would continue our drive and set up camp right where the PCH goes right back to the coast. We would camp on the beach there, giving us a full day to drive up the coast. Perfect. Santa Barbara was only an hour north of us, and we planned on getting more engagement photos there. So even with all my panic of feeling as though we needed to rush ourselves, I was beginning to realize we were actually running in excellent time.

As we all climbed back into the van, we sat in our unofficially assigned seats, Bobby and I had been sharing the burden of driving, except Bobby had been doing most of it up to this point. I decided since it was his first time in California, I would try to do as much driving up the coast that I could, so he could focus on the scenery.

"I feel so conflicted." Bobby said after several minutes of traveling. "I look to the right and I'm like 'Whoa! Look at those mountains!' but then I look to my left and I'm like 'Whoa! Look at that ocean!' This is awesome!" We then passed through some pasture where cows grazed on the grass all the way up to the edge of a cliff overlooking the ocean. "Wow, I could seriously live out here and do some farming. Dad wouldn't have any trouble convincing me to take over *this* farm."

It almost seemed unfair how these cows had such beautiful scenery to live in. They must be the cows they talk about when they say "happy cows are from California." If I was one of those cows, I would be happy, too.

After several miles of beautiful scenery, we arrived in Santa Barbara with plenty of daylight to spare. The last time I was there was with Cameron and two other recent graduates, slacklining between the palm trees near the beach.

The sun was still high, allowing us plenty of time to slow down and enjoy the area. It was exactly as I remembered it. Palm trees lined along the street with plush grass beneath them. Just beyond the trees laid a sidewalk where people could walk or ride bike parallel to the ocean. Next to the sidewalk was plenty of sand leading right into the ocean. The ocean waters had gentle waves, but nothing sizeable. It almost seemed as though we were right up against a large lake on a windy day.

Cara got right to it with her camera as Larissa and I walked toward different places to have photos taken. Cara was in full photographer mode as we walked toward a palm tree. After snapping several photos she guided us to the pier, where we posed for different photos underneath. As we continued on with our primary engagement photoshoot, Bobby and Cameron goofed around while exploring the area. Larissa and I were having lots of fun trying different things and being creative with our photos, peeking from behind pillars of the boardwalk, as well as several other fun poses. I even tried hanging upside down so my head was right at her level. Attempting to do so was more difficult than I thought it was going to be, since I hadn't been climbing quite as regularly and wasn't in as good of shape as I was used to being in.

Larissa and I then proceeded to get photos together above the boardwalk. As the sun was setting and darkness was taking over, we were ready to wrap up our photoshoot. Just as we were about to head to our van, the lights came on for the pier. The color of the lights were a typical off-white glow, but they were strung together like Christmas lights raised 10 feet above the side of the pier. We took advantage of the beautiful backdrop and posed for a few more photos with our new inspiration.

We were feeling satisfied with the numerous pictures we had taken, and we knew we had several upcoming photographic opportunities to take advantage of. One place in particular we were looking forward to was Pfeiffer Beach, a beach Bobby Brett told us we certainly needed to visit.

Being early in December, there weren't any tourists around besides us. Even the locals weren't spending any time outside in the perfect night air. As we walked around the dimly lit streets of Santa Barbara, we stumbled upon a carousel in the park. The carousel was fully lit up with all the features of a classic carousel. Oddly enough, nobody was around. Nobody at all. It was just us. I asked the attendant if it was open. Of course it may seem obvious, but it certainly seemed odd there was nobody riding it, and maybe it wasn't worth operating unless there was a large number of people willing to ride. He said it was open and it would be $2.00 per person for a ride. Under normal circumstances I would have considered it a waste of money, since there isn't much excitement in riding a carousel. However, there was an enormous appeal for us to go for a ride since we had a chance to have the entire thing to just the five of us.

We hopped on board and each got on a horse. Larissa and I rode side by side as Cara was ahead of us snapping photos. The carousel played music while our horses gently moved up and down while the entire machine spun us around in circles, barely slow enough to prevent me from getting sick. (Even as an adrenaline junkie, motion sickness is my downfall.)

After what felt like an impressively long time, the carousel slowly came to a stop and our ride had come to an end. It was certainly worth it, considering I wouldn't expect to have such a privilege of having it all to ourselves ever again.

As our evening was beginning to get late, we needed to make sure we could visit Michelle in San Luis Obispo before it was too late. After getting in touch with her, we set out to meet up at the coffee shop where she was studying for her college classes. It only took us about an hour for us to get there, and the driving was mostly inland, so we didn't feel as though we were missing too much scenery. When we arrived, we found the coffee shop to be full of college students and hipsters. The tables and chairs were old fashioned with several outlets available for charging cell phones and laptops. The room was uniquely lit by lamps casually hanging upside down from the ceiling. The shop was designed to embrace the current hipster culture, as well as complement the needs of college students.

Our time visiting with Michelle was very enjoyable. She was very excited to see Larissa again and gawk at her flashy, new engagement ring. We told her about our experiences so far on the trip, and caught up on her life as well. Our visit lasted maybe an hour, which went by very quickly. As much as we all wanted more time to visit, she needed to get back to her studying, and we still had yet to figure out where we would be sleeping that night.

We parted ways and climbed into the van as we continued on our adventure. As Bobby drove, I used my phone to view google Earth to try and locate a beach we could camp on. I managed to find a place called Morro Bay, located right where the PCH joined along with the coast once again. It would be the perfect place for us to begin driving in the morning. Morro Bay featured a large rock face protruding from the earth called Morro Rock, which would be an easy landmark for us to find, even in the dark.

As we pulled into the parking lot of where our chosen campsite was, I looked at the weather on my phone. 36 Degrees Fahrenheit. It was going to be a cold one. Especially cold for California. This wasn't the kind of weather I was hoping for. I was expecting it to be peaceful and a comfortable 60 degrees. We would stay up sharing stories, and fall asleep comfortably situated on the sand, with the soothing sound of the ocean to listen to as we rested.

This was the furthest thing from what I had in my mind, but I was adamant about sticking to our original plan. Fortunately, I had come prepared with my 20 Degree mummy bag and several articles of warm clothing, including two pairs of my techwick long underwear, wool socks and a warm base-layer long sleeve shirt, as well as a hoodie to go overtop. I was prepared for the worst, and this was certainly close to it. We parked and I stepped outside, only to be startled by the conditions we would be facing. The wind was cold and fierce, blowing straight through the clothes I was wearing. Cameron and Cara had come prepared with a warm sleeping bag they had borrowed. As an early Christmas present, I had given Larissa a nice cold weather North Face sleeping bag that would surely get her through the night easily. Bobby pulled out the sleeping bag he had packed. It looked like the kind of bag I was sent to summer camp with when I was in Elementary School. It was in no way, shape or form, made to be used in these brisk conditions.

I was genuinely concerned for his well being and I offered to lend him some of my warm clothes. I only brought so much with me in case somebody needed something extra.

Bobby pridefully turned down my offer. "I'll be alright," he said confidently. I strongly urged him once more to borrow some of the clothes I had brought. He adamantly told me he didn't need any extra clothes and he would be just fine.

The plan was for all of us to sleep out on the beach. Naturally, we would keep ourselves segregated. Bobby was there, so he would be sure Larissa and I had more than enough space apart so that even Jesus would approve. Larissa and Cara weren't feeling well, so they decided to fold the seats down in the van and turn it into their own personal hotel room. With the extreme wind and bitterly low temperatures, I wasn't about to try and convince them to join us on the beach. Besides, Larissa had lost her voice from being so sick and still wasn't showing any signs of recovery.

As soon as Bobby, Cameron, and I had our layers on and sleeping bags ready to go, we boldly marched our way out onto the sand. The wind was blowing sand all over the beach to the point we needed to squint as we walked. Each of us wore a headlamp to light the path in front of us. The light on our head highlighted the grains of sand flying horizontally across our faces.

Once we were close enough to hear the ocean over the sound of the wind, we chose to set up camp right where we were. As I pulled my sleeping bag out of it's case, the wind was blowing so hard my sleeping bag was flailing horizontally like a windsock in a hurricane. I pinned it to the ground and opened the zipper so I could start the complicated process of getting into it without bringing sand along with me. I took my shoes off one at a time, working my feet into the bag without directly touching the cold sand. The sand was absorbing the cold temperatures just as much as it absorbs heat on a hot summer day.

When I finally worked my way entirely into the sleeping bag, I zipped it up as much as I could and pulled the strings around my face tight so I could see only a little bit out of the mummy hole. The wind violently blew sand against my sleeping bag, but for the most part it was remaining airtight. This night was turning more and more into a fight for survival rather than the enjoyable night out under the stars with the sound of ocean waves as I had imagined it would be.

Bobby and Cameron had crawled into their sleeping bags as well. While Cameron was doing his best to stay warm, Bobby could feel the cold air blowing straight through his sleeping bag and through the few layers of clothing he was wearing. We all decided to move closer together to try and block the wind best we could without being close enough to be legitimately spooning. We felt as though we had entered into survival mode as we made our best attempt to fall asleep. I kept my face away from the wind that was coming at me. Even though my fancy mummy bag only had a small hole of exposure, sand was still getting inside. It was surprisingly difficult to breathe without getting sand in my mouth. I wasn't quite warm enough to feel comfortable, but it was good enough to get some sleep in these near-freezing temperatures.

I struggled to fall asleep as the wind continued howling loudly. My face was becoming irritated with the sand that was blowing into my mummy bag. As I forced myself to fall asleep, I felt as though as I was going in and out of consciousness.

While I was managing to get only a little bit of rest, I was the only one lucky enough to do so. Cameron got up and walked back to the van so he could sleep along the side of it where the wind would be blocked off for the most part. Not too long after he sat against the tire nodding off, a police officer pulled into the parking lot to kick people out who were camping. He asked Cameron a series of questions, and eventually told him we needed to get out of the parking lot since camping was prohibited. He gave him a recommendation on where we could go to park for the night and camp.

Cameron headed back to the beach, through the blowing sand toward me and Bobby. "Hey, the cops are here, we need to go." Cameron said as I was still fast asleep.

"Good!' Bobby exclaimed as he leapt out of his sleeping bag. He was freezing, and on the verge of hypothermia and was more than happy to get up and go to the van. "Tom," he said abruptly waking me up, "we gotta go, we've got cops." He said loudly in my face so I would hear his voice over the sound of the wind, and through all the layers I had around me.

Though I still felt half asleep, I started mentally preparing myself to get out of my cocoon, put my shoes on and head to the van. I unzipped the bag and looked around. Bobby was already nowhere to be seen. I was all by myself. I noticed how the blowing sand had formed a drift up against my body as I crawled out and put my shoes on after dumping the sand out that had settled in them. I put my headlamp on and made my way back to the van with my sleeping bag flailing in the wind as I walked.

When I got back to the van and placed my gear in the trunk, Bobby was packing things in as he shivered uncontrollably. "It's so cold. I'm so glad we're leaving. I love cops. It's so cold." He was saying as he climbed into the driver's seat. Bobby was literally on the verge of hypothermia. He was muttering sentences that didn't make complete sense as he started the van so he could blast the heat as soon as the engine warmed up.

All the seats were back in their upright position. Cameron was on the bench seat in the back, the girls were in their seats in the middle, Bobby and I were in the front ready to go. The girls had overheard Cameron talking to the cop when he was there. He had given directions on a good place for us to park and camp for the night.

"Cameron, where did the cop tell us to go for the night?" Cara asked him.

"Yeah, I really don't know. I was really cold. I just nodded my head and agreed with everything he said to me." He replied.

"So you don't remember anything he said as to where we should go?" Cara inquired further.

"Up the road? That way?" Cameron said as he pointed. So now we really weren't sure on where we were supposed to go. It was 2:00am and we were going to have to find somewhere suitable to park and rest.

We drove north a few minutes and pulled into a parking lot that seemed as though it would be acceptable. We parked in a spot facing the ocean. None of us were motivated to make another attempt to sleep outside. We all just reclined in our seats, doing our best to get any rest we could.

Bobby sat upright in his seat looking out at the ocean. The waves were enormous and when they crashed it sounded like thunder in the distance. "Whoa." Bobby said with big eyes. "Did you see that? These waves are huge. Holy cow. Did you see that one?" Bobby was still shivering and trying to get himself warm again.

As we all remained in our seats attempting to get any rest we could, Bobby continued babbling on about how big the waves were while he continued to shiver. Eventually he was able to warm back up and fall asleep as well.

The next morning we were awakened by the sunlight. Bobby talked about how he had never been so cold in his life. He's an incredibly tough guy and he can take on a lot of pain and miserable circumstances, but for him to talk about how cold he was gave the cold night all the credit it needs.

Fortunately, Bobby had walked the fine line of hypothermia without crossing it, so the day ahead of us was looking good. We had a list of several beautiful places to see before we would be spending the night at Glenda's, sleeping in actual beds. We certainly looked forward to catching up with her and the kids, as well as catching up on our sleep.

As we drove north on the PCH, we shared our stories from our sad attempt to camp out. Bobby talked about the enormous waves he could see when he parked the van after we were kicked off the beach. I remember they looked pretty large, but Bobby was describing them as so much more massive than I was remembering. I called him out for being delirious from hypothermia.

Pretty soon we encountered the Piedras Blancas Elephant Seal Rookery; an area Cameron and I had stopped to see on our last trip. It was the home of dozens upon dozens of Elephant Seals. They were scattered all over the beach. These seals didn't get their name by mistake, either. These bad boys can get up to twenty feet long and weigh up to four tons. It is very difficult to comprehend until you see them for yourself. When these seals would move their enormous mass, ripples from their fat move through their entire body. After spending several minutes observing and getting photos of these freaks of nature, we proceeded on our way.

We had two places we wanted to be sure to see. McWay Falls, and Pfeiffer Beach. Both of which were easy to miss. (Easy enough that Cameron and I didn't see them the last time we were on the PCH). The weather was beautiful. It was sunny and clear, relatively warm, and it was pleasantly comfortable wearing just a T-shirt. This felt like the California I was used to.

We continued north as we climbed hills in the van, driving along the cliffside looking down at the ocean. Large rocks were scattered below, protruding from the water, as the waves were crashing among them. We pulled over at several different places to get photos and appreciate the scenery. The most difficult part was managing our time and not stopping at every single pull-off.

Once we arrived in Big Sur, we kept our eyes out for McWay Falls and Pfeiffer beach. After we finally came across a small and subtle sign for Pfeiffer beach, we followed the long driveway down to a parking area. We climbed out of the van and found a small path in between some trees towards the beach. After we passed through the trees, it opened up to an incredible beach. Straight ahead of us were two enormous masses of rock. They were a beautiful light brown color. In the middle of each of them was a hollow cave going directly through them, also referred to as the "Keyhole" where the waves crashed through. Beyond these masses of rock were waves that had to be at least 12 feet high crashing from left to right in a perfect tubular motion.

Everything about this beach was beautiful. It was just as much, if not more incredible than what Robert Brett had described it to be. I could see why he enjoyed coming here to take pictures. Cara was already snapping away capturing as much of the beauty as she could. Larissa and I walked toward the Keyhole of the closest rock, skipping across a few rocks to avoid getting our feet wet. Below us in the water were beautiful clusters of seagrass and clams.

Larissa and I ventured as close to the keyhole as we could without getting too much salt water on our clothes. It was incredible to see the waves crashing right through the keyhole in the rocks. We posed for Cara as she snapped away photos of us as she kept an eye out for any possibility of water getting anything more than our feet wet from an oncoming wave.

Meanwhile, Cameron and Bobby explored the area, climbing around on some of the rocks, and taking in the different views. Both of them were blown away by the beauty of this secluded beach as well. We were very fortunate that in this month of December, we had this heavenly place entirely to ourselves.

After Cara had snapped several beautiful engagement photos, Larissa and I walked back onto the sand, exploring more of this secluded area. Cara continued snapping photos of waves crashing through the keyhole, as well as the different small plants growing in the water. She was practically in heaven as she wandered around the beach capturing anything worthy of a photo, which was pretty much everything in sight.

As much as we wanted to stay there for the rest of our lives, we had to make sure we had a chance to find McWay falls and check it out, since it was bound to be another beautiful location. We walked through the plush sand, towards the path that lead us back to the van.

I searched on my phone to find out where McWay falls was. With poor service it took a long time to load, but when it finally did, we found out we had overshot it by about 12 miles. Awesome. The GPS said it was a half hour south of us, so this was going to add at least an hour of driving by backtracking to see it. All of us decided regardless of the extra time it would take us, it was worth seeing. Additionally, we would be able to stop at a coffee shop we had driven past, which featured an incredible ocean view. Ever since we had passed it, we were wishing we had taken the time to relax and enjoy beverages in the open air, overlooking the ocean.

As we drove southbound, we came across the coffee shop. The Coast Gallery & Cafe was conveniently located right along the PCH. Even though we were slightly pressed for time, we wanted to slow down and enjoy every moment we were blessed with.

After ordering our drinks, we all sat around a table on the top deck, joking and laughing about various things. The sun was high in the sky, it was a clear day, and we were on a rooftop overlooking the Pacific Ocean far below us. Life was good. It was the kind of moment that made you wish life could stay that way and never change. The weather couldn't be more perfect, we were surrounded by some of our best friends, and I was engaged to a girl more incredible than I could have ever imagined.

After we finished our beverages, we got back in the van and headed just a little further south to McWay falls. When we arrived at the parking lot, we got out and walked through a tunnel under the road towards the designated overlook. The size of the waterfall wasn't very impressive. It was a relatively small stream of water, but it still looked incredibly beautiful as the water dropped onto the sand below as waves washed up on the shoreline. The water in the cove was a beautiful turquoise color that had an abrupt change to a darker blue as it merged with the open sea.

There was no walkway down to the beach, and a sign clearly stated that nobody was allowed to go beyond the fence where we stood. It was truly unfortunate we were restricted from being able to go down to the beach below, but from our distant vantage point, the scenery was still difficult to fathom. Cara snapped away with her camera, capturing the beauty of this easy-to-miss location. The beauty was so vast, it was difficult capturing it all in a single frame. Turning around for this treasure was absolutely worth it.

We walked back to the van and started driving north again. If everything went smoothly, we were expecting to make it to San Francisco with a little bit of daylight, and then proceed to Roseville to see Glenda and the kids.

The final stretch toward San Francisco wasn't disappointing. The scenery continued to be an assortment of rocks, cliffs, and ocean that continued endlessly. The highway weaved as it ran parallel to the shoreline. After an hour of navigating northward, the PCH started taking us inland toward San Francisco. Being as late as it was, we were fortunate to be there while we still had some daylight. We didn't have much time to spend, but we had all the time we needed, since the Golden Gate Bridge was the only landmark on our agenda.

After slowly driving through city traffic, we finally made it to the bridge. We drove across as we admired the beauty of the incredible architecture. After we crossed, we took the first exit to a scenic overview so we could get out and take pictures. I had been to San Francisco a couple of times before and one thing I found interesting was how the fog was so confined to the San Francisco Bay area. There was plenty of fog surrounding the bridge, but we were fortunate enough to see at least most of it.

It was difficult to believe how cold it was, considering we were comfortable in our T-shirts earlier in the day, but now we were wearing our hoodies and winter jackets, while still shivering.

It didn't take long for us to run out of things for us to see. It was a beautiful bridge, but there wasn't much more to expect from it. Besides the fact that we were cold and soon to be out of daylight, we wanted to get to Glenda's as soon as we could.

One reason I was making sure we got there at a decent time, was the fact that they were celebrating Taylor's 16th birthday. We wanted to be there for it so we could surprise her, since both she and Trevor weren't told we would be coming. As we got back on the road to continue our travels, I texted Glenda to give her an update on when to expect us, since we were only two hours away.

When we arrived, I pulled up to the gated entrance for her neighborhood. I typed in the code Glenda had given me and the gate swung open allowing us to enter. I pulled through and immediately to the left was the house. It was a very large spanish style home, with beautiful green grass, and a cement wall surrounding the backyard and saltwater pool. The interior of the home was equally as impressive.

Glenda came outside to greet us and helped sneak us inside. Once we walked in, Taylor and Trevor gave us enormous hugs, as they were overjoyed we came to see them. They asked Larissa and I if we were actually married or not. They were full of enthusiastic curiosity with everything they had seen on Instagram. We shared the story with them briefly, and I asked if they were surprised to see us. They said they were a little, but given the fact that we were in California, they had a hunch we would be coming to visit.

The rest of that night, we celebrated Taylor's birthday, eating delicious food as we shared stories from our trip up to that point.

Over the next few days, we were able to unwind and relieve the stress that we had been under from our travels. Glenda was a magnificent host as usual. She took us out to eat multiple times, and she even took us out to play some laser tag!

Since we had a few days to relax, we wanted to be sure to call our family and close friends to share the wonderful news about our engagement. We started with our family and friends who had been making an effort to contact us. Several of them had left us voicemails and sent us texts, making an effort to wish us a congratulations on what they were thinking might have been a wedding. Some of them were reaching out simply to find out what exactly was going on.

After Larissa and I had a chance to call several of our friends and relatives, we put the first update on facebook since the fake elopement. We announced that we were engaged and updated our relationship status as well. The congratulations from our friends rolled in quickly, along with the comments about the approach we had taken, and how confusing it was to them.

After enjoying a couple days of visiting, relaxing, and having fun in Roseville, we knew we had to fly out of Las Vegas the next night.

Glenda, Bobby, Cameron, Cara, Larissa and I gathered around the granite countertop of the island in the kitchen and discussed our options.

The initial plan for this part of the trip was to drive to Yosemite, take some photos there and check out the park, before proceeding to Las Vegas for our flight. We were calculating the time it would take to drive, how much time we would have at Yosemite, and how much wiggle room we had in that plan. In order to be able to even accomplish this, we would have to leave incredibly early in the morning. Stupid early. And even then, we didn't have much room for error. I didn't want us to miss our flights, or cut it as dangerously close as we did on our first date. If we didn't go to Yosemite, we would be well rested, be able to say goodbye to Taylor and Trevor, and have plenty of time to drive to the airport.

It would have certainly been quite logical to fly out of Sacramento, but the flights in Vegas were far less expensive, and renting a vehicle can be far more costly if you don't return it to the same location.

We considered leaving immediately and driving through the night, but that would certainly set each of us up to be far too exhausted upon our return home. After much discussion, we all decided it would be a wiser decision to drive straight to

Vegas and skip Yosemite. It certainly was a hard decision, and I hated for Cara to feel let down as well, since she was really looking forward to getting photos of the beautiful National Park.

The next morning, we woke up early enough to see the kids before they left for school. We said our goodbyes, and shortly after they had left, we were packed and ready to go. Glenda wished us well along with a final congratulations as we left. We exited through the gate and started heading south.

The next several hours were relatively uneventful. Bobby drove as I kept my eyes out for another In-N-Out Burger to stop at for a bite to eat. Meanwhile Bobby did his best to distract me from any billboards featuring where the next one would be. At this point he was growing very tired of In-N-Out, since I made a point to go there at least once every day.

After we had finally driven far enough south to reach Interstate 15, we were able to feel like we were heading in the right direction. East. Going from Sacramento to Las Vegas is somewhat awkward, since there really isn't a direct path to get there.

Along the way we had lots of fun goofing off. Singing songs, partying, recording videos and taking pictures. Anything to keep ourselves occupied. We were carrying on so much to the point Bobby nearly rear-ended a tractor trailer in the slowed traffic, almost giving us all a heart attack.

We kept cruising right along making excellent time. Cruising along just a little too well, actually. It was dark, and we had been driving for a long time. When Bobby has been driving for a long time, apparently he drives relatively fast. We flew by a California Highway Patrol Officer sitting in the shadows of an underpass at a pretty quick pace. "That was a cop.." Bobby muttered as he took his foot off the gas. We watched behind us to see if the officer was going to come after him. Sure enough, we see him turn onto the freeway and catch up to us with little effort. As cops tend to do, he paced behind us for about 10 seconds before flicking his lights and siren on. Larissa began to freak out. "Oh crap, we're going to get a ticket. I just know it." she said as all of our hearts began to race.

"Don't worry, guys." Bobby stated confidently. "I've got this. Just stay calm."

As we waited for the officer to walk up to us after we had pulled over, Bobby was feeling confident he would be able to talk his way out of it, since he was a Deputy at the jail near Atlanta.

The officer approached the passenger side of the vehicle as we rolled down the window for him. The look on his face wasn't very friendly, not that we expected it to be. Since I was in the passenger seat, I was the one directly in front of his face. I did my best to say little as possible so I could give Bobby the chance to talk his way out of this one. I really didn't have anything to worry about, myself.

"Hello officer, how are you doing today?" Bobby asked cautiously.

"Is there any reason you were going so fast back there? I clocked you at 92." The officer began the interrogation immediately, establishing his dominance without beating around the bush.

"Honestly officer, I wasn't paying as much attention to how fast I was going as I should have been." Bobby started off. "I'm a detention deputy at a county jail in Georgia, and I know I should know better than to be driving so fast. I'm really sorry, I should have used better judgement."

Bobby handed over his driver's license as well as his badge. Bobby was making sure to take full advantage of the fact that he was a Deputy.

"What are you guys doing in here California?" the officer inquired as he inspected Bobby's Georgia license. I knew this was my chance to step up to the plate with a little bit of convincing on why we shouldn't get a ticket. After all, when you just became engaged, who wants to be the one to rain on your parade?

"Well, I put this trip together so I could actually propose to my fiance back there." I stated, as Larissa smiled awkwardly while flashing her shiny new engagement ring.

"I see. Well, congratulations." He stated kindly without breaking out of character. "Let me look a few things over and I'll be right back."

When the officer got back into his vehicle, all of us gawked at the fact that Bobby got caught doing 92. We debated over whether he would be getting a ticket or not. Bobby was pretty convinced he wouldn't be. All of us were convinced otherwise.

After the cop came back to the van, he was kind enough to issue Bobby an official warning. He wished us well on the rest of our trip and told Bobby to slow it down. Bobby thanked the officer with every bit of sincerity. After the cop walked back to his cruiser, Bobby's look of sincerity turned into a big grin. "Told you guys I'd get out of it."

From the backseat of the van Cameron chirped in with an innocent childish voice "Thank you, Uncle Bobby for being a Sheriff's Deputy!"

We all bursted out in laughter as Bobby merged back onto the freeway. I glanced at the GPS on my phone to see how we were doing on time. Getting pulled over was a bit of a setback, but we were still in excellent shape. It wasn't going to hinder our ability to board our flights on time. At least we didn't have that to worry about.

Maybe a half hour later on our drive, we encountered a little bit of debris on the roadway. It wasn't much, but it was small enough that by the time we saw it, it was already too late to react. There was a light "thump" as we drove over it. It didn't sound good at all, but it could have been much worse. A few minutes went by and the "Low Tire Pressure" symbol appeared on the dash.

"Tom," Larissa said "I think we need to pull over somewhere and make sure everything is okay. Look, there're some gas stations right over there. Bobby, take this exit." Cara backed her up and encouraged us to take the exit.

"Don't worry about it." I said. "I'm sure it's just some kind of slow leak coming from the tire. I mean, we've put about 3,000 miles on this thing. We'll be fine. Just keep driving, Bobby." I didn't feel there could be much wrong. After all, I had been dealing with a slow leak in one of the tires in my Subaru for a long time. I was sure it was something similar to that effect. Besides, we were in good shape to arrive at the airport at a good time. I didn't want to jeopardize the excellent time we were making.

A few minutes later we started hearing a noise coming from the tire. Bobby looked over to me with an I-think-the-girls-were-right look on his face. "Tom I think we need to take a look at this tire." He said.

"Take this next exit," I told him in agreement. "Pull into the nearest Gas Station."

Bobby exited the freeway about a half mile later. The noise was getting increasingly worse, as our fears were becoming realized more and more with every passing minute. By the time Bobby pulled into the gas station there was no denying the fact that we were driving on a tire that had no air.

The gas station was poorly lit. An old car sat nearby with a windshield that was shattered, most likely by vandals. This didn't look, sound, smell, or feel like a safe place at all. Larissa couldn't help but mention how we had passed the safe-looking, well-lit gas station we had seen from the freeway when she told us we should pull over.

We got out of the van to see what we were dealing with. The tire was completely flat with no hope of retaining air. There was a long slit in the sidewall where the tread was separated completely from the tire. We needed to get a spare tire on as quickly as possible.

We sprung into action pulling the luggage out of the back of the van, only to find there wasn't a spare tire there. We looked around the vehicle best we could to figure out where the spare tire might be. I knew if we were able to get the tire on right away, get on the road, and head to the airport, we would still be borderline of making it time if we drove only a little faster than what you're supposed to with a spare tire, but this was all cutting it too close to be comfortable.

As we searched unsuccessfully for the spare, my gut had the returning feeling of when Larissa and I had almost missed our plane. Except now, there were five of us returning to three different airports, which could turn into a logistical nightmare.

Since we weren't having any luck finding a spare tire, I called the rental company. I was beginning to think the car might need towed and we would need a replacement rental car to get us back. After talking to a representative, I was transferred to someone who had mechanical knowledge about the van we had rented. This helpful gentleman informed me the spare tire was stored underneath the van and instructed us to remove the center console, which exposed a nut. We loosened the nut using the crowbar we retrieved from the back of the van. As Bobby loosened it we all watched underneath as a spare tire was lowered down from the dead center of the van.

I unhooked the tire and pulled it out. Meanwhile, Bobby was already in the back grabbing the jack. As Bobby set up the jack, I loosened the lug nuts with the crowbar, working quickly and efficiently as a team. Once Bobby jacked up the van, we swapped out the flat for the spare in no time. As we tightened the lug nuts and lowered the van, Cameron inspected the flat tire, immediately finding a drill bit pierced into it. At least we now knew exactly what had happened.

We threw the tire in the back and piled the luggage on top of it. Bobby immediately got us back to the freeway as we headed towards Las Vegas. We had about two hours of driving ahead of us, and we couldn't even do the speed limit, according to the recommendations of the tire we were driving on. Last thing we needed was to blow another tire. There would be no recovering from that. We were cutting it close. Very close. We couldn't afford any more mishaps. We weren't even sure if we were going to make it as it was. The driving that followed involved a lot of nervous silence. It was difficult to be enthusiastic when we were all worried about missing our flights.

Cara broke the nervous silence and got our minds off the situation by asking us about the health of our spiritual lives.

Her question brought on enriched conversation about devotions, church, and our daily habits. She then led us in prayer that we would make it to our flights on time, and that we could get there safely as well.

Finally, after a couple of nerve-wracking hours, we were right outside of the airport in Las Vegas. If we were fast, we would hopefully make it to our flights on time, but there was no room for error. None at all.

We drove into the rental return and parked the car where it instructed, leaving the keys inside. I quickly explained to them about the tire and signed a damage report in acknowledgement. We grabbed our things as we all dashed to the shuttle busses which would transport us to our designated terminals.

We all said our goodbye's as Bobby and Cara each had separate terminal busses to get onto. Bobby's flight was scheduled to leave the next morning. He was already planning to sleep on a bench somewhere in the airport. He couldn't even go through security and sleep in the terminal since he was more than 12 hours early for his flight. Larissa, Cameron and I took the bus to our terminal. If everything went right, we would make it in time, but there wasn't much time to spare.

As soon as we stepped off the bus, we grabbed our bags and jumped in line to have them checked. Once the bags were checked and we had our tickets, we swiftly made our way to security. The lines weren't too terribly long as we made it through effortlessly. After we were through and had our carry on's, I looked at the time. We had twenty minutes to spare. I could finally breathe as we walked to our terminal knowing we would be able to catch our flights.

CHAPTER 12
God's Perfect Love Story

Our return to Pennsylvania didn't turn out to be quite the heroes-welcome I was hoping for. My anticipation was that my family would overlook the fact that I took time away from the farm unannounced and recognize that it was for the greater good of putting together an epic proposal for Larissa. My parents were glad that we were now engaged, but my practical jokes tend to be too much for them to handle. A couple years prior while working on a stunt driving gig in Boston, I posted a photo on Facebook of my realistic-looking makeup that made me look as though I had serious wounds on my head and chest. Since I was playing the part of an accident victim, it was too easy to have my family convinced that I had been in a serious car accident on my way there. When people texted me to ask what had happened I told them I had an accident and I had a bruised heart, two broken ribs, a fractured sternum and a punctured lung. The thing that likely made this practical joke far less humorous to my parents was the reality of the car accident that should have taken my life when I was 17. Fake eloping as another practical joke was a pretty tough one for them to handle, since I was prone to doing something so wild.

I offered my apologies to my uncles who were also a part of the farm for taking the time off. I hoped they would understand my position when I explained it to them so I could make light of the situation. They still came down on me pretty hard, laying on a guilt trip, followed by a brief "Congratulations". I was pretty bothered by how upset they allowed themselves to be about it, since there really isn't much work happening on a farm in December. I could only imagine the reaction I would have received if we had gone through with the plan in September, as we originally planned.

Larissa and I decided not to allow these things to bother us and to do our best to enjoy this time in our life. We decided we would be getting married 7 months later on June 21, 2014. There was plenty of work ahead of us for planning out the wedding, it was insane. Save the Dates, invitations, finding a location, deciding on music, dresses, tuxedos, flowers, and the list went on and on and on.

While Larissa had her focus on the wedding, I was mostly looking forward to what would be taking place after the wedding: The Honeymoon, and of course, having sex. I had grown up being taught that I needed to save myself for marriage. I was taught that not only is it what God wants for us, but also that there was the dangers of STD's, and the difficulties that can come with an unplanned pregnancy.

To be honest with you, Larissa and I were determined to save ourselves for our wedding night, but nobody was direct and upfront with us about how difficult that would be. It seems as though it should be easy. "Don't have sex". "-Okay!". But the fact is, the temptation is there, and it is as strong as you allow it to be. Even though we managed to save ourselves for our wedding night, Larissa and I allowed the temptation to be much stronger than it should have been. Our relationship was filled with kissing, and it would run our emotions very high. Not just when we were dating, but also when we were engaged. We would be watching a movie, and all of a sudden, we're making out. We're doing more wedding planning, and again, we're suddenly making out. I'm not going to lie; I'm pretty sure I'm the one who initiated it just about every time. Making out was awesome. Getting physical felt awesome. It was great to have someone who made me feel so wanted, but I do wish I would have handled temptation differently before we were married.

As enjoyable as it can be, making out can make it extremely difficult to keep your hands where they belong and stop pushing the boundaries any further. It's like allowing a large ball of snow start it's way down a mountain. It's only just a little. You could stop it at any point you want, right? But when that snowball starts rolling, it's gaining momentum, and it's getting larger, and more difficult to stop. Just like when getting physical, it becomes more and more difficult to say "no" as the temptation gets stronger and stronger. You start getting more comfortable with the things that you used to feel were really borderline of what you considered to be acceptable.

Every passing week of our relationship the temptation to have sex grew stronger and waiting for our wedding night became ever increasingly difficult. It was especially challenging since we knew we would be getting married. The date was set, the invites, were out, and we were soon to be committed to spending the rest of our lives together. I want to be upfront with you: When you're at that point in life where you have found the right person, the battle becomes incredibly fierce. Satan will plant all kinds of lies into your mind and give you reasons why you don't need to wait. He tries to have you convinced that waiting as long as you have is "good enough" or "you're going to marry them anyhow, so why wait?"

So why should we still wait even when you've found "The One"? Well, you're still not married! As I had mentioned earlier in this book, I had girls in the past who I thought were "The One". Of course I fell easily, and I fell hard. It was pathetic, really. In my life, I've seen engagements break up, and of course I've seen several other people convinced they found "The One" as well. I'm sure you can think of a person who declared they've found "The One" with every relationship they get into! Fact is, God wants us to save ourselves for our spouse, and they're not a spouse until the vows have been exchanged. You know what else? It's worth the wait! It really is!

I remember waking up on my wedding day with a feeling of accomplishment. As though I was on the verge of completing the most difficult challenge I had ever faced. The challenge of preserving myself for my wedding day. The challenge of preserving myself so I could give my soon-to-be wife the best gift I could possibly give her. A gift that could only be given once. To one person. Ever. Knowing that I would be giving myself to my wife that night felt liberating.

I'm not going to go into detail about how things went down that night in our hotel, but something incredible happened. We shared something new. We shared something that neither of us had shared with any other person. This was just between us. It was exciting, fun, and an entirely different adventure for each of us. We had finally made it. We had conquered the strongest temptation we had ever faced in our lives and we felt more than just a sense of accomplishment. We felt we were fulfilling what God desired for us. The exclusive intimate bond between spouses.

One of the greatest things about our first night together was knowing that God was smiling with approval. This is how He intended it to be. Not only was that night passionate, and completely mind-blowing for us, but we experienced freedom from any guilt-ridden feelings we would have had otherwise. We knew this was what God wanted and we were fulfilling His desires by being intimate as husband and wife.

Another incredible aspect was that there was no competition. Since this was the first time for both of us, I didn't have to feel as though I was being compared to anyone, and she didn't have to feel that way either. It wasn't about outperforming anybody. I didn't feel as though I had anything to prove. It was about sharing an incredible passion and being completely intimate with each-other. Knowing this was something we shared only between ourselves made it all the more incredible and exclusive.

It is difficult for me to express how blessed I am to have the opportunity to share the feelings involved with being intimate for the first time, and what it is like to share the experience with the same person for a lifetime. Unfortunately, not too many people are privileged enough to say they have done the same. They trade the experience God wants for them for a more self-serving, sub-standard version of what they would call intimacy. An intimacy without commitment. It breaks my heart to see so many young teens and adults who fall into temptation, and miss out on the incredible gift that God has for them. I see examples of this all the time.

So many people don't realize why God gives us these instructions. One thing I've come to conclude from my own experience, is that God doesn't just want us to obey Him as a way of honoring Him, but He wants us to have the best sex possible! He wants us to enjoy this gift with someone we are truly in love with. He doesn't want to see us go through the pain of giving ourselves intimately to someone only to experience the sense of loss and disappointment when the hookup, fling, or dating relationship is over!

Sometimes I ask myself why I've decided to write this book. I don't consider it to have been a decision, but more of a calling. When God calls us to do something, it's our obligation to make a conscious decision and follow His calling. I'm not even an author, to be honest with you. Even if this book turns out to be any form of a success, I still wouldn't call myself one. I never had any desire in my life to write a book in my life and I don't want to write one ever again. The fact is, God gave me and Larissa an incredible love story, and I can't help but feel compelled to share it with you. I pray that I can be fulfilling the plan He set out for me to the best of my ability.

God has an incredible love story designed specifically for you. Odds are very slim that it involves whisking someone away across the country, but if you pursue His desire for your love life, you'll be amazed at how He can tailor a love story directly to your wants and needs, and who you are as a person. I happen to be a spontaneous risk taker who learned what God wanted to teach me at just the right time for me to meet the woman I now call my wife.

Sometimes I look back and think about how I could have done things differently, and there is certainly a long list. I feel as though I wasted so much time when I was single just hoping, watching, waiting, and keeping my eyes peeled for my future wife to come waltzing through the door. I wasn't trusting in God's plan. I wasn't trusting God with my love life at all.

I'm convinced my day-to-day life would have been better if I had quit worrying about who God would bring into my life, and focus on where God had me in life. I should have been putting forth my best effort to trust in His plan.

I was fortunate enough to be a Young Life leader and positively influence dozens of young teenagers. My co-leader, April, often talked about how panicked the disciples were as a squall swept over the lake and the disciples were convinced they were going to drown. They woke Jesus (who was fast asleep), and He mocked the storm and calmed the waters. The challenging thought was how different the storm would have been for the disciples had they thoroughly trusted Jesus through the harsh winds and magnificent waves. What if they trusted in the fact that they weren't going to die, since they had the Son of God on the boat with them, and they just enjoyed it, and rode the waves as if it was an adrenaline pumping boat ride?

I spent so much of my teen and young adult life in a panic, with no trust in the fact that God had it all figured out.

I wish I had been confident enough to trust in God whole-heartedly with my love life instead of stressing so much about it, or even giving it much of a thought. Had I trusted Him all along, I would have been able to make more out of every moment, focusing on where God had me, instead of where I wanted God to have me. I'm so thankful God had given me a change of heart just before I met Larissa. I was full of confidence in God's plan for my life, and excited in wherever it would take me. Even if I would be single for the rest of my life.

So what if I hadn't met Larissa? What if God had in fact, designed me to be single for the rest of my life? Where would I be now? I'd like to believe I would have been able to continue with the complete contentedness I was feeling in the week prior to meeting Larissa and in the time I was getting to know her. I would like to believe I'd be having a blast with whatever God had in front of me. Would I still be leading Young Life? Would I be skydiving? BASE jumping, even? I don't know where I would be. But I know if God had intended me to be single for the rest of my life, it would only be as awesome as I would allow Him to make it.

Honestly, there are several things I would like to have done differently in our relationship too. Sure, the first date and the proposal were full of adventure and more fun than I could have imagined possible, but there's several parts in between the adventure I feel I could have been more honoring to God, and have more purity in our relationship.

We certainly had lots of fun going on several dates, and having lots of movie nights, but temptation was constantly knocking at the door trying to convince us to give ourselves to each-other and just have sex. Caving into temptation and having sex would have certainly been the easy way out, but it would have made our wedding night and honeymoon far less special. There are several things God taught us about resisting temptation and self-control. Those are two vital characteristics needed in every marriage. When you hear about an unfaithful spouse, what characteristics are the individual lacking? The ability to resist temptation, and an application of self-control! Saving ourselves for marriage not only preserves our purity, but it also equips us for the strength to withstand temptation we face when we're married.

Here's something I was never told that I want to pass onto you: Saving yourself for your future spouse is likely to be the most difficult, yet rewarding things you will ever do. Don't let your guard down and assume it's going to be an easy task. The temptation is incredibly strong, especially when you're in a serious relationship. If you allow yourself to be placed in tempting situations, it will be all the more difficult. I heard all around the church and at Christian events about how you need to save yourself for marriage, but I don't recall anybody being blunt enough with me about how difficult it is. It will likely be one of the most difficult challenges in your life, but I promise you, the trials are necessary to build you into a stronger relationship with God, and your future spouse. Additionally, I promise you, it's worth the wait. God lays down His commands because He wants the best for you, and He wants you to experience the best! The way God designed it is to be nothing less than the best!

Even though Larissa and I didn't have sex until our wedding night, we allowed temptation to knock at our door far too often. I know for a fact we certainly spent too much time alone. I wish we would have made more of an effort to hang out with friends more often. Group events are more awesome than you realize. Take the fake elopement for example. There wasn't a single moment where I felt temptation knocking at my door. The thought never even crossed our minds. We were too busy having so much fun as a group. When you're around friends, it's so much easier to focus on having fun and getting to know one another without the temptation to have sex or get physical. As weird as it sounds, the trip would have been much less fun if it was only me and Larissa doing all that traveling without accountability. We could have certainly been putting ourselves in a situation with more temptation than we could handle.

In this day and age, saving sex for marriage seems to be extreme. But I know some people who didn't even kiss until their wedding day. Now THAT's intense! It really sounds far out. But is it really? In all seriousness, that is something I wish I had the courage to do. Making a decision of how much temptation you want to resist is like deciding whether it's easier to stop a boulder from starting to roll down a hill versus stopping a boulder that is currently rolling down the hill ready to destroy everything in it's path. My first kiss with Larissa felt perfect in the moment, and it was in a very romantic setting, but I feel resisting temptation to kiss would have been so much easier to resist than the temptation we were facing to have sex. Not to mention, speaking as Larissa's husband, I look back at how I was as a boyfriend and if I had a chance, I would slap myself for not respecting Larissa as much as I could have. I'm so thankful we saved ourselves for marriage, but I know we could have done better to remain pure.

I can even think back to how it would have been easier to stay pure when I was single. It's insane how much we are all sexualized by the media. It's almost impossible to go a day without temptations of lust to be displayed around us, causing us to think sinful thoughts. One eye opening experience I had, in regards to this, was when I was on the road trip to California with Cameron and the other guys who had just graduated high school. We spent several days just driving from one national park to another, finding random places to camp every night. We were so busy enjoying nature, away from the world, away from the media, that about four days into our trip, I suddenly realized that I hadn't felt any temptation or even had a lustful thought, which was nearly impossible to comprehend how that could even happen. This caused me to realize how much the media really affects us, filling us with impure thoughts and desires. It's easy to see how the impurity of the media has a negative effect on our generation.

There are several changes I would make if I were to be in my teens and young adult years again. First thing I would do is get rid of my smartphone. I'm thankful I didn't have one until half a year before I was married. You don't have to go far on a smartphone to stumble across sexualized images. They commonly pop up on apps like Instagram and Snapchat. Beyond that, access to a world of pornography is at the palm of your hand. I'm glad I didn't carry this temptation with me everywhere I went.

Second thing I would do is be extremely particular about what movies and TV shows I watched. Honestly I almost feel hypocrital writing this. There's a lot of TV shows and movies I really love. TV shows like Friends or That 70's show. They're great, and very entertaining, but one thing they do is treat sex as if it's a casual everyday thing. As if it's just what you're supposed to do. It easily convinces your subconscious that casual sex is perfectly fine. You never want to underestimate the effects the media can have on you. The world doesn't hesitate to lie to you.

The third thing I would do is have a close friend keep me accountable. I was recently having a meeting with my friend Jarren about a business I run, and he received a random text from a friend boldly asking him if he's staying pure and avoiding pornography. The text was direct and straight to the point. It was awesome to see that he had a friend that cared enough about him to keep him accountable. Purity is a difficult struggle, even when you're single. I encourage everyone to find a close friend to keep them accountable in purity not only when you are single, but especially when you're in a relationship. For obvious reasons, don't designate the person you're in a relationship with to keep you accountable. In fact, make sure your accountability partner is the same sex. They will understand what you face at a deeper level and know how to help you better than anybody else.

When I was getting my motorcycle license, I took a motorcycle safety class. The instructors were very clear in the beginning. "You will ride motorcycle the same way you drive a vehicle. If you take stupid risks when you drive a car, you're bound to take the same stupid risks, and possibly kill yourself on a motorcycle." They said sternly. This shook me up, considering I had wrecked my Mitsubishi Lancer *and* my Mazda RX-8 within six weeks of each-other not long before I took the class. Had the instructors known that, they would have kicked me out of class right there and then. Sure enough, I eventually did wreck my motorcycle. I was fortunate enough to walk away. Or hobble away, at least.

Just like my transition from driving a car to riding a motorcycle, exercising the ability to resist the temptation of lust when you're single will carry over to when you're in a relationship. Think what you do on your own isn't going to affect the way you handle temptations of lust when you're in a relationship? Think again. You're going to cave into temptation just as easy in a relationship as you do when you're single. Resisting temptation is a muscle you need to exercise daily, and just like a muscle, as you exercise, your ability to resist temptation will get stronger. The best way to equip yourself to resist temptation in your life when you are single or in a relationship is to have God at the center of your life, and your relationship. Strengthen your relationship with Him by reading devotions and spending time with Him in prayer.

Remember that your relationship with God is like any other relationship. If you're dating someone and you stop talking to them, how do you expect the relationship to last? Likewise, if you stop praying, and stop reading the Bible, how would that affect your relationship with Him? I've been heartbroken seeing friends of my own allow their relationship with God dwindle and drop it entirely because they're not "feeling" His existence in their life. I continue to pray for these friends daily.

As I finish this book that I have felt compelled to write, I want you to know that I'm not here to tell you how to run your life. You're entitled to make your own decisions. But I wanted to share with you how awesome it is that my wife and I decided to pursue purity in our relationship and save ourselves for marriage.

One thing I didn't want to focus on in this book was to write about the consequences of premarital sex. I could focus an entire chapter on the risks of sexually transmitted diseases, or the challenges of an unplanned pregnancy. There's enough people in the world who can share with you the detrimental effects of premarital sex. I wanted to focus on the rewarding side of following God's plan.

The fact is, I'm incredibly blessed to share with you the joy that comes with purity in a relationship. I'm one of the few in my generation who are able to express how beneficial it is to experience God's gift of sexual romance with only one woman. She is not only my best friend, but I'm lucky enough to spend the rest of my life with her.

Purity is what you make of it. You can choose to keep yourself as pure as you want, and you will have so much, or so little to give your future spouse, depending on the choices you make when you are single or in a relationship. I just want you to know how thankful I am for my choice to be pure. I'm so blessed to have a God who brought me to the realization that I needed to trust in Him in all I do, in whatever may or may not happen in my life and in my relationships. Not only did He give me peace about what could have been, but He gave me what my heart truly desired ten-fold! I never thought I would have this kind of story to tell. It all still amazes me how God brought all of these pieces together.

One last surprising detail about the story I share with Larissa is the list she wrote years before she met me. It was a list of characteristics she desired in a future spouse. Ironically, a week after she met me, she stumbled upon the list she had forgotten about while going through an old book. The folded up list fell out and onto her lap. The list is written verbatim as follows:

If I marry….
　　The things I hope my husband will be….

1) Funny. He <u>HAS</u> to have a sense of humor.
2) Nice eyes. Not creepy…. (like glossy, perve eyes)
3) Has to know how to dress. -Be able to wear a tie.
4) -Disclaimer- Larissa skipped #4. Idk why.
5) Stronger than me. (Cause I'm pretty tough…)
6) Taller. Even when I wear heels. No girl wants to be a freak.
7) Know how to drive… fast and well. -Have a bike.
8) Be adventurous. (not afraid to try new things.)
9) Likes to cook. (so I don't have to ALL the time)
10) Be a gentleman w/o smothering me or my independence.
11) Allows me to have fun.
12) Doesn't judge me for my awesomeness, but rather embraces it.
13) Understanding. -Willing to listen
14) HAS to love cats. -_- or at least MY cats.
15) Not Amish
16) Isn't stuck in some far off time zone.
17) Good looking would be a plus…
18) Kind, caring, humble, receptive, loving, gentle, patient.
19) Doesn't hog the bed. (That's my job)
20) Not afraid of hard work.

21) Stubborn. In a good way... (Like Peter... in the Bible.)
22) Please, please, <u>Pleeeease</u> be older than me....
23) AWESOME. Not boring and crabby.
24) Has to make me laugh.... And be able to laugh with me.
25) I'm halfway to 50. This should be enough to anyone who reads this.
THIS WASN'T MY IDEA!

25B.)
In all seriousness...
<u>Even</u> <u>if</u> <u>He</u> <u>isn't</u> all those things...
He <u>Has</u> to <u>Love</u> <u>God</u>. By that I mean, <u>Love</u> <u>God</u> - REALLY. Love <u>God</u> <u>More</u> <u>than</u> <u>he</u> <u>loves</u> <u>me</u>. End of story.

26!) Oh. AND he has to love kids. If not...
Sorry... NO CAN DO.
"Hit 'da road, Jack...."

What are the odds Larissa would have a list put together of what she wanted in a future spouse years before we met, and that list described me perfectly? Well, with the God we have the odds increase quite exponentially. God wants to give us what we want in a future spouse. The coolest thing you can do is ask for it. I challenge you to make a list of the important qualities you want in a future spouse, just like Larissa did, and pray about it. Keep it tucked away somewhere hidden so you can revisit it when you're in a serious relationship. Don't compromise your standards.

Psalm 37:4 says "Take delight in the Lord, and He will give you the desires of your heart." I remember quoting that verse when I was single and waiting for the Lord to fulfill the desires of my heart, which were obviously to find a wife and get married. God brought Larissa into my life not when I expressed the desire, but when I finally wanted what God wanted for my life more than what I wanted for my life. I was given the desires of my heart not long after I truly and completely was taking delight in the Lord. I'm not listing this as any kind of a magical formula. God's timing is different for every person. The best you can do is trust God's timing, as well as His direction for your life, no matter where that may be. I can tell you, if you trust God completely, and let Him guide you in every direction of your life, He'll give you a story more incredible than you could have come up with on your own.

It might not be a story that takes you across the country, but it will be exactly what God wants for you. A story designed specifically for you. And you'll still be likely to consider it the craziest thing.